A GUIDE TO

A GUIDE TO

ARCADIA

SHAUN McCARTHY

WITH TONY BUZAN

Hodder & Stoughton

ISBN 0 340 80302 9

First published 2001
Impression number   10 9 8 7 6 5 4 3 2 1
Year   2006 2005 2004 2003 2002 2001

Cover photograph: Donald Cooper, Photostage
Illustrations: David Ashby
Mind Maps: Kate Boyd

Typeset by Transet Limited, Coventry, England.
Printed in Great Britain for Hodder & Stoughton Educational, a division of
Hodder Headline Plc, 338 Euston Road, London NW1 3BH by Cox and Wyman Ltd,
Reading, Berks.

CONTENTS

You are now in the most important educational stage of your life, and are soon to take English Literature exams that may have a major impact on your future career and goals. As one A-level student put it: 'It's crunch time!'

At this crucial stage of your life the one thing you need even more than subject knowledge is the knowledge of *how* to remember, *how* to read faster, *how* to comprehend, *how* to study, *how* to take notes and *how* to organize your thoughts. You need to know how to *think*; you need a basic introduction on how to use that super bio-computer inside your head – your brain.

The next eight pages contain a goldmine of information on how you can achieve success both at school and in your A-level English Literature exams, as well as in your professional or university career. These eight pages will give you skills that will enable you to be successful in *all* your academic pursuits. You will learn:

◆ How to recall more *while* you are learning.
◆ How to recall more *after* you have finished a class or a study period.
◆ How to use special techniques to improve your memory.
◆ How to use a revolutionary note-taking technique called Mind Maps that will double your memory and help you to write essays and answer exam questions.
◆ How to read everything faster while at the same time improving your comprehension and concentration.
◆ How to zap your revision!

How to understand, improve and master your memory of Literature Guides

Your memory really is like a muscle. Don't exercise it and it will grow weaker; *do* exercise it properly and it will grow incredibly more powerful. There are really only four main things you need to understand about your memory in order to increase its power dramatically:

Recall during learning
– *YOU MUST TAKE BREAKS!*

When you are studying, your memory can concentrate, understand and recall well for between 20 and 45 minutes at a time. Then it *needs* a break. If you carry on for longer than this without one, your memory starts to break down. If you study for hours non-stop, you will remember only a fraction of what you have been trying to learn, and you will have wasted valuable revision time.

So, ideally, *study for less than an hour*, then take a five- to ten-minute break. During this break listen to music, go for a walk, do some exercise, or just daydream. (Daydreaming is a necessary brain-power booster – geniuses do it regularly.) During the break your brain will be sorting out what it has been learning and you will go back to your study with the new information safely stored and organized in your memory banks. Make *sure* you take breaks at regular intervals as you work through the *Literature Guides*.

Recall after learning
– *SURFING THE WAVES OF YOUR MEMORY*

What do you think begins to happen to your memory straight *after* you have finished learning something? Does it immediately start forgetting? No! Surprisingly, your brain actually *increases* its power and carries on remembering. For a short time after your study session, your brain integrates the information, making a more complete picture of everything it has just learnt. Only then does the rapid decline in memory begin, as much as 80 per cent of what you have learnt can be forgotten in a day.

However, if you catch the top of the wave of your memory, and briefly review what you have been revising at the correct time, the memory is stamped in far more strongly, and stays at the crest of the wave for a much longer time. To maximize your brain's power to remember, take a few minutes and use a Mind Map to review what you have learnt at the end of a day. Then review it at the end of a week, again at the end of a month, and finally a week before the exams. That way you'll surf-ride your memory wave all the way to your exam, success and beyond!

The memory principle of association

The muscle of your memory becomes stronger when it can **associate** – when it can link things together.

Think about your best friend, and all the things your mind *automatically* links with that person. Think about your favourite hobby, and all the associations your mind has when you think about (remember!) that hobby.

When you are studying, use this memory principle to make associations between the elements in your subjects, and thus to improve both your memory and your chances of success.

The memory principle of imagination

The muscle of your memory will improve significantly if you can produce big images in your mind. Rather than just memorizing the name of a character, imagine that character of the novel or play as if you were a video producer filming that person's life. The same goes for images in poetry.

In *all* your subjects use the **imagination** memory principle.

Throughout this *Literature Guide* you will find special association and imagination techniques (called mnemonics after the Greek goddess Mnemosyne) that will make it much easier for you to remember the topic being discussed. Look out for them!

Your new success formula: Mind Maps®

You have noticed that when people go on holidays, or travel, they take maps. Why? To give them a general picture of where they are going, to help them locate places of special interest and importance, to help them find things more easily, and to help them remember distances and locations, etc.

It is exactly the same with your mind and with study. If you have a 'map of the territory' of what you have to learn, then everything is easier. In learning and study, the Mind Map is that special tool.

As well as helping you with all areas of study, the Mind Map actually *mirrors the way your brain works.* Your Mind Maps can be used for taking notes from your study books, for taking notes in class, for preparing your homework, for presenting your homework, for reviewing your tests, for checking your and your friends' knowledge in any subject, and for *helping you understand anything you learn.* Mind Maps are especially useful in English literature, as they allow you to map out the whole territory of a novel, play or poem, giving you an 'at-a-glance' snapshot of all the key information you need to know.

The Mind Maps in the *Literature Guide* use, throughout, **imagination** and **association**. As such, they automatically strengthen your memory muscle every time you use them. Throughout this guide you will find Mind Maps that summarize the most important areas of the English Literature guide you are studying. Study these Mind Maps, add some colour, personalize them, and then have a go at making your own Mind Maps of the work you are studying – you will remember them far better! Put them on your walls and in your files for a quick and easy review. Mind Maps are fast, efficient, effective and, importantly, *fun* to do!

HOW TO DRAW A MIND MAP

1 Start in the middle of the page with the page turned sideways. This gives your brain more radiant freedom for its thoughts.

2 Always start by drawing a picture or symbol of the novel or its title. Why? Because *a picture is worth a thousand words to your brain.* Try to use at least three colours, as colour helps your memory even more.

3 Let your thoughts flow, and write or draw your ideas on coloured branching lines connected to your central image. The key symbols and words are the headings for your topic.

4 Next, add facts and ideas by drawing more, smaller, branches on to the appropriate main branches, just like a tree.

5 Always print your word clearly on its line. Use only one word per line.

6 To link ideas and thoughts on different branches, use arrows, colours, underlining and boxes.

HOW TO READ A MIND MAP

1 Begin in the centre, the focus of your novel, play or poem.

2 The words/images attached to the centre are like chapter headings; read them next.

3 Always read out from the centre, in every direction (even on the left-hand side, where you will read from right to left, instead of the usual left to right).

USING MIND MAPS

Mind Maps are a versatile tool – use them for taking notes in class or from books, for solving problems, for brainstorming with friends, and for reviewing and revising for exams – their uses are infinite! You will find them invaluable for planning essays for coursework and exams. Number your main branches in the order in which you want to use them and off you go – the main headings for your essay are done and all your ideas are logically organized!

Super speed reading and study

What do you think happens to your comprehension as your reading speed rises? 'It goes down!' Wrong! It seems incredible, but it has been proved – the faster you read, the more you comprehend and remember!

So here are some tips to help you to practise reading faster – you'll cover the ground much more quickly, remember more, *and* have more time for revision and leisure activities!

SUPER SPEED READING

1 First read the whole text (whether it's a lengthy book or an exam paper) very quickly, to give your brain an overall idea of what's ahead and get it working. (It's like sending out a scout to look at the territory you have to cover – it's much easier when you know what to expect!) Then read the text again for more detailed information.
2 Have the text a reasonable distance away from your eyes. In this way your eye/brain system will be able to see more at a glance, and will naturally begin to read faster.
3 Take in groups of words at a time. Rather than reading 'slowly and carefully' read faster, more enthusiastically. Your comprehension will rocket!
4 Take in phrases rather than single words while you read.
5 Use a guide. Your eyes are designed to follow movement, so a thin pencil underneath the lines you are reading, moved smoothly along, will 'pull' your eyes to faster speeds.

HOW TO MAKE STUDY EASY FOR YOUR BRAIN

When you are going somewhere, is it easier to know beforehand where you are going, or not? Obviously it is easier if you *do* know. It is the same for your brain and a book. When you get a new book, there are seven things you can do to help your brain get to 'know the territory' faster:

1 Scan through the whole book in less than 20 minutes, as you would do if you were in a shop thinking whether or not to buy it. This gives your brain *control*.

2 Think about what you already know about the subject. You'll often find out it's a lot more than you thought. A good way of doing this is to do a quick Mind Map on *everything you know* after you have skimmed through it.

3 Ask who, what, why, where, when and how questions about what is in the book. Questions help your brain 'fish' the knowledge out.

4 Ask your friends what they know about the subject. This helps them review the knowledge in their own brains, and helps your brain get new knowledge about what you are studying.

5 Have another quick speed read through the book, this time looking for any diagrams, pictures and illustrations, and also at the beginnings and ends of chapters. Most information is contained in the beginnings and ends.

6 If you come across any difficult parts in your book, mark them and *move on.* Your brain *will* be able to solve the problems when you come back to them a bit later. Much like saving the difficult bits of a jigsaw puzzle for later. When you have finished the book, quickly review it one more time and then discuss it with friends. This will lodge it permanently in your memory banks.

7 Build up a Mind Map as you study the book. This helps your brain to organize and hold (remember!) information as you study.

Helpful hints for exam revision

◆ To avoid **exam panic** cram at the *start* of your course, not the end. It takes the same amount of time, so you may as well use it where it is best placed!

◆ Use Mind Maps throughout your course, and build a Master Mind Map for each subject – a giant Mind Map that summarizes everything you know about the subject.

◆ Use memory techniques such as mnemonics (verses or systems for remembering things like dates and events or lists).

◆ Get together with one or two friends to revise, compare Mind Maps, and discuss topics.

AND FINALLY ...

◆ *Have fun while you learn* – studies show that those people who enjoy what they are doing understand and remember it more, and generally do better.

◆ *Use your teachers* as resource centres. Ask them for help with specific topics and with more general advice on how you can improve your all-round performance.

◆ *Personalize your* **Literature Revision Guide** by underlining and highlighting, by adding notes and pictures. Allow your brain to have a conversation with it!

Your *amazing brain and its amazing cells*

Your brain is like a super, *super, SUPER* computer. The world's best computers have only a few thousand or hundred thousand computer chips. Your brain has 'computer chips' too, and they are called brain cells. Unlike the computer, you do not have only a few thousand computer chips – the number of brain cells in your head is a *million MILLION*!! This means you are a genius just waiting to discover yourself! All you have to do is learn how to get those brain cells working together, and you'll not only become more smart, you'll have more free time to pursue your other fun activities.

The more you understand your amazing brain the more it will repay and amaze you!

Apply its power to this *Literature Guide*!

(Tony Buzan)

OW TO USE THIS GUIDE

This guide assumes that you have already read *Arcadia*, although you could read 'Context' and 'The story of *Arcadia*' first. It is best to use the guide alongside the play. You could read the 'Characterization' and 'Themes' sections without referring to it, but you will get more out of these if you do.

THE SECTIONS
The 'Commentary' section can be used in a number of ways. One way is to read a scene of the play, and then read the relevant commentary. Keep on until you come to a test section, test yourself – then have a break! Alternatively, read the Commentary for a scene, then read that scene in the play, then go back to the Commentary. See what works best for you.

'Critical approaches' sums up the main critical views and interpretations of the play. Your own response is important, but be aware of these approaches too.

'How to get an "A" in English Literature' gives valuable advice on what to look for in a text, and what skills you need to develop in order to achieve your personal best.

'The exam essay' is a useful 'night before' reminder of how to tackle exam questions, though it will help you more if you also look at it much earlier in the year. 'Model answer' gives an example A-grade essay and the Mind Map and plan used to write it.

THE QUESTIONS
Whenever you come across a question in the guide with a star ✪ in front of it, think about it for a moment. You could make a Mini Mind Map or a few notes to focus your mind. There is not usually a 'right' answer to these: it is important for you to develop your own opinions if you want to get an 'A'. The 'Test' sections are designed to take you about 15–20 minutes each – time well spent. Take a short break after each one.

PAGE REFERENCES
Note that page references are to the 1993 Faber edition. They may vary slightly for any other edition.

KEY TO ICONS

Whenever a **theme** – a key idea explored in the play – is dealt with in the guide, an identifying icon is used. This means you can find where a theme is mentioned by flicking through the guide. *Arcadia* is a play about ideas, and, with the exception of 'sexual attraction', its themes are intellectual rather than emotional.

Six key themes or ideas running through the play are identified with icons in the 'Characterization' and 'Commentary' sections. They are explained in more detail in the 'Themes' section.

Fact and fiction		Ambition	
Sexual attraction		Arcadia	
History		Art versus science	

Thought versus feeling: the Age of Enlightenment and the Romantic Movement.

The age of Enlightenment was a European philosophical movement of the eighteenth century, mainly founded on the seventeenth-century Scientific Revolution, and on the ideas of philosopher John Locke and philosopher-scientist Isaac Newton. Its basic belief was the superiority of reason as a guide to all knowledge and human concerns. The thinkers of the Enlightenment believed in progress achieved through scientific knowledge and new understanding.

The Romantic Movement could almost be seen as a reaction to the rational enquiry and logic of the Enlightenment. It is not the same as (modern) romantic writing! It was a radical, far-reaching shift in thinking in the late eighteenth and early nineteenth centuries, which affected the whole of human understanding and experience. Romanticism focused on the importance of the individual. Personal experience and emotion replaced logic as the most important driving forces in human existence.

The Romantic Movement was partly based on the work of philosophers (such as Berkeley, Hume and Kant), but it was the imaginative writers of the period, the novelists and poets, who really developed the ideal of individualism that would inspire so many people. As a literary movement, Romanticism was extremely powerful in England. Among the most important writers associated with it are the poets Wordsworth, Coleridge, Blake, Keats, Shelley, and of course Byron.

Some modern critics claim that there are few writers who bear no trace of this profound revolution in thought and feeling, and that Romanticism is one of the major influences on the modern age.

Landscape gardening

Landscape gardening, on the grand scale carried out at Sidley Park, is the art of laying out gardens and estates for aesthetic or spiritual effect. The sort of gardening we imagine going on beyond the windows of the set of *Arcadia* is on a huge scale. Lady Croom has lakes, streams, bridges and vast sweeps of parkland and woods for Noakes to play with. The garden she so loves is a rolling country park laid out by **'Capability' Brown** (1715–83).

In reality Brown was probably the most famous English landscape gardener. Many stately homes have parks designed by him. He acquired his nickname by telling clients that their gardens had excellent 'capabilities'.

Humphrey Repton (1752–1818) was a successor to 'Capability' Brown. He completed the change from the formal gardens of the early eighteenth century to the 'picturesque'. Today 'picturesque' means vaguely 'as pretty as a picture', but in the eighteenth century the term was much discussed as an aesthetic style, somewhere between 'beautiful' and 'sublime'. 'Picturesque' was applied mainly to rugged landscapes with rocks, waterfalls, and winding paths – the sort of thing Noakes wants to construct.

In scene 2 Hannah refers to an earlier garden design at Sidley Park, much more geometric and neat in its design. This style was more in the spirit of the Enlightenment, during which it was constructed. These gardens would have had formal gravel walks, carefully shaped trees and bushes, and orderly flowerbeds in strict geometrical patterns. This is the *Paradise in the age of reason* (page 27) that Hannah has seen in an engraving and wishes had never been destroyed.

So the gardens at Sidley Park go through three phases:

1 The formal garden that was torn up before Lady Croom's time.
2 The rolling parkland garden of 'Capability' Brown that is still there in 1809.
3 The rugged picturesque landscape being built by Noakes in 1812.

Byron: a brief biography

One of the most famous and popular English poets of all time, George (Gordon) Byron, 6th Baron, known as Lord Byron (1788–1824) spent his first ten years in poor surroundings in Aberdeen. Then he inherited the title of his great-uncle, and went on to Harrow public school (where Stoppard imagines he met Septimus), and Cambridge. An early collection of poems, *Hours of Idleness* (1807), was badly reviewed, and he wrote the satirical 'English Bards and Scotch Reviewers' to poke fun at those who were *considered his seniors and betters* (as Chater comments on page 40). He toured Europe from 1809 to 1811, then returned to England and growing public acclaim. In 1812 he was in London, often in the company of Lady Caroline Lamb (1785–1828). She was the wife of William Lamb, an MP who went on to become Prime Minister. Although she was a successful novelist, she is often best remembered for her nine-month public infatuation (1812–13) with Lord Byron. It caused a great scandal.

So Stoppard has set the play at exactly the point in Byron's life where a scandal could have forced him to flee abroad. Byron could have left for Europe in 1809 because he had killed Chater, and he was in London with Caroline Lamb in 1812, when Lady Croom and Septimus see him at the Royal Academy.

Byron enjoyed great fame and popularity as a heroic and romantic poet, but he was ostracized by 'polite' society in England because he was suspected of having a more than brotherly love for his half-sister Augusta Leigh. He again went to Europe, where he met Shelley, another great Romantic poet, and spent two years in Venice. Some of his best works belong to this period. He gave active help to the Italian revolutionaries, and in 1823 he joined the Greek freedom-fighters who had risen against the Turks who occupied their country. He died of malaria at Missolonghi, Greece. The Greeks thought Byron a great romantic hero, and until recently his portrait still appeared on matchboxes!

Science in Arcadia

Most of the science you need to know in order to understand the play is explained in the text, usually by Valentine. The core of the idea with which Stoppard is working is that Thomasina was a child who saw, almost effortlessly, a key problem with Newtonian physics that eventually led thinkers and scientists to formulate the second law of thermodynamics, which is one of the cornerstones of physics. Although you only really need to know that Thomasina was extremely clever, a little understanding of the complexity of the theories she grasped so easily will add depth to your understanding of her character and of the times in which the play is set.

Sir Isaac Newton (physicist and mathematician, 1642–1727), had done ground-breaking work on physics over a hundred years before Thomasina was born. His laws of motion and theories of heat and energy were accepted as true accounts by almost everyone who had any interest in science. But during the early years of the nineteenth century, scientists began looking at the problem of heat lost in motion. What Thomasina reads in the French journal may be an early article on this matter. But the idea which she effortlessly sketches, based on the inevitable loss of energy in Noakes's steam pump, would not be completely formulated by scientists as the second law of thermodynamics until much later in the century.

Thermodynamics is the study of heat and heat-related phenomena. It is based on four fundamental laws, but we only need worry about the second one, the one Thomasina presents to everyone in the final scene. Technically, it can be expressed in full as: 'a law giving direction to thermodynamic processes in time, and thus forbidding some which would otherwise be allowed by the First Law'. It may be expressed in several equivalent ways:

1 No heat engine can have a thermal efficiency of 100 per cent, i.e. it is impossible to convert heat totally into mechanical work; for example, car engines and power stations can never be 100 per cent efficient, no matter how well they are built.

2 No process may have as its only outcome the transfer of heat from a cold object to a hot one; for example, a refrigerator requires power to make an object at room temperature cold, whereas a cold object will warm up to room temperature on its own.

3 A system will always finish in the state which can be realized in the greatest number of ways; for example, a drop of ink in water will finish up dispersed evenly through the water since this corresponds to the greatest number of arrangements of ink and water atoms.

4 For a closed system, entropy is either constant or increasing.

Before the nineteenth century, heat was thought to be a material substance, termed 'caloric'. Hot objects were thought to contain more caloric (hot substance) than cold ones, and an object's supply of caloric was limited. The modern conception, that heat is a form of energy, and that heat flow is energy transfer, was originally suggested by Count Rumford in 1798. Conservation of energy was first understood by Sadi Carnot in 1830, and was developed by James Joule in 1843, and others. Notice the dates: Thomasina might have been reading something by or about Count Rumford, but she was developing ideas similar to those of Carnot and Joule, who will not 'catch up' with her discoveries for another twenty or thirty years. And remember that Thomasina is only 13 at this point in the play!

Septimus Hodge is tutor to the only daughter of Lord and Lady Croom. He educates her in the school room of their great country house, Sidley Park, which is surrounded by 500 acres of gardens. The entire play is set in this room, though the time setting moves between 1809, 1812 and the end of the twentieth century.

The play skilfully mixes comedy with a tragic ending. This mood is set up in **scene 1** when we hear Septimus and Thomasina in a lesson. They discuss Fermat's theorem – and the subject of sex, more like friends than tutor and pupil. They are interrupted by Ezra Chater, a poet who is staying at Sidley Park with his wife, as guests of Lady Croom's brother Captain Brice. Septimus has been seen having sex with Mrs Chater in the garden. Ezra Chater wants to fight a duel, but Septimus talks him out of the idea: Chater is easily fooled.

They are joined by Lady Croom, Brice and Noakes, the landscape gardener, who is commissioned (against Lady Croom's will) to redesign the garden. He wants to make a new 'picturesque' style of garden to replace the rolling parkland. There is much confusion between gardening and sex in the garden, which only Thomasina seems able to put straight. She already seems to be the cleverest person in the play!

Scene 2 takes us into the modern day. Hannah Jarvis is researching the history of the gardens at Sidley Park. Chloe, Valentine and Gus are the daughter and sons of the estate's present owners, the Coverlys. University historian Bernard Nightingale arrives. He wants to meet Hannah to see if they can collaborate on historical research. He won't give his real name because he wrote a bad review of Hannah's last book, on Caroline Lamb, a woman who became infatuated with poet Lord Byron.

Hannah and Bernard spar with one another. They are both professional debaters. Bernard has evidence to suggest that Byron stayed at Sidley Park in April 1809, and that he fought a duel with Chater, killed him and fled the country. Hannah is suspicious of Bernard, especially when she finds out who he really is. Despite this, she agrees to let him work alongside her.

Chloe is attracted to Bernard. Valentine seems only mildly interested in Bernard's appearance in his house. He is more interested in Hannah, but they don't seem to have any sort of real relationship.

Scene 3 returns to 1809, and Thomasina struggling with a Latin lesson. They drift into a discussion of a mathematical idea that Thomasina has worked out, but which Septimus doesn't appear to give much credence. They move on to discuss ancient history and the classical world. The friendly, light-heartedly intellectual atmosphere is destroyed when Chater and Brice arrive. Chater has discovered that it was Septimus who gave his last book such a dreadful review. This additional insult is driving Chater to renew his demand that Septimus fights a duel.

There is much comedy caused by the fact that Septimus seems to regard the idea of fighting as a joke. They are interrupted by Lady Croom, who tells Septimus to lend Byron his copy of Chater's new book. She takes it with the various notes (unsigned and unaddressed) to Septimus still inside it. These are going to lay the false trail that tricks Bernard so many years later. When Lady Croom has gone, Septimus becomes angry and say he will fight duels with both Chater and Brice.

In **scene 4** Hannah has found Thomasina's mathematical ideas. Valentine tells her it is a valid and unusual type of calculation but he doesn't believe a schoolgirl in the early nineteenth century could have found it out. He describes the research he is doing, and says that the sort of complex maths into which Thomasina just might have had an insight could never have been proved without a computer.

Bernard bursts in claiming to have found evidence to prove his 'Byron killed Chater then fled' theory. Hannah warns him to be careful because there are too many holes in his theory, but Bernard is driven by a lust for professional fame. The scene closes with an empty stage and a distant pistol shot: has a duel in fact been fought?

In **scene 5** Bernard is reading his lecture to Chloe, Valentine and Hannah. He has arranged media coverage of his great discovery but Hannah is still not convinced that he has enough evidence. She is still quietly looking for the identity of the Sidley Park hermit who lived in a hovel in the garden as a sort of living ornament for over twenty years in the early nineteenth century. He apparently filled his hovel up with wild mathematical calculations.

Valentine and Hannah will not accept Bernard's theory. He becomes angry, and an argument over the relative values of scientific knowledge (Valentine) and artistic experience (Bernard) becomes heated and personal. When Valentine withdraws close to tears, Bernard just says, *It's no fun when it's not among pros is it?* He seems blind to the upset he has caused at Sidley Park. But, before leaving, he admits to having seduced Chloe, makes a half-hearted attempt to do the same with Hannah, then gives her some information she needs about her hermit. Valentine returns and tells Hannah that some of the ideas the hermit was apparently struggling with were to do with the second law of thermodynamics, a theory that had not yet been discovered in the period Hannah is researching.

For **scene 6** we go back to the empty stage and pistol shot of early morning 1809. It turns out to have been Septimus shooting rabbits. There has been no duel. Lady Croom discovered Charity Chater sneaking out of Byron's bedroom (it is suggested Lady Croom might have been trying to sneak in). She has thrown out Brice and the Chaters, and Byron has also gone. She is planning to send Septimus after them, but in the course of their interview, Septimus manages to declare his passion for Lady Croom. The scene ends with her ordering him to come to her room later that evening.

The long **final scene** combines characters and action from both time-frames of the play on stage simultaneously. Valentine and Chloe are reading newspaper headlines reporting Bernard's discovery, and discussing the deterministic view of the universe. Valentine shows Hannah what he has done with Thomasina's mathematics and a powerful modern computer. It works – showing that she did understand the idea of endlessly repeating iterated algorithms.

Thomasina enters the schoolroom with her brother, Lord Augustus. They are in high spirits. She is now on the eve of her 17th birthday, and the enthusiasm and energy that she has shown up to now burn even more strongly. Septimus admits for the first time that he has missed the ideas she has been exploring in her work. She is almost casually exploring the ideas that form the basis of the second law of thermodynamics.

Valentine and Hannah discuss the same theory. Hannah begins to believe there was a genius living in the house in 1812, but she is not sure whether it was Septimus or Thomasina. They mention a girl who was accidentally burned to death on the eve of her birthday. Augustus and Septimus argue, and Thomasina spins off away from cutting-edge science to wondering if Lord Byron will marry her, and then to having Septimus teach her to waltz for her birthday.

Lady Croom describes the dwarf dahlias, the first in the country, that Brice has sent back from the Indies. He took the Chaters with him on a voyage of botanical discovery. Ezra Chater has been killed and Brice has married his widow. Lady Croom criticizes the damage being done to her garden by Noakes, and particularly condemns the noise of the steam engine he has installed as a water pump. Thomasina uses the pump as a way of explaining the second law of thermodynamics that she has discovered. No one really understands her genius.

Augustus returns and apologizes to Septimus. He asks to be told the 'facts of life'. Bernard returns like a hunted animal. Hannah has told him what she has discovered about the dwarf dahlias at Sidley park. They prove that Chater was not killed there. She plans to make her discovery public and suggests that Bernard should back down quietly and admit his mistake. He goes off to a fancy-dress ball that is about to take place in the grounds of the house.

Septimus is reading alone late at night when Thomasina enters in her nightgown. She wants him to teach her to waltz. While they wait for Count Zelinsky to play suitable music on the piano in the next room, Septimus reads Thomasina's essay on thermodynamics. So does Valentine in the twentieth century.

He realizes the girl really was onto something quite monumental. He is explaining what Thomasina saw to Hannah when Thomasina and Septimus begin to waltz.

A frantic Bernard arrives, pursued by a tearful Chloe. They have been caught together in the hermitage by Chloe's mother. Bernard leaves.

Septimus has kissed Thomasina. She wants him to come to her room. He tells her to be careful of the candle flame: she is the girl who is burned to death. They begin another waltz. Gus enters and gives Hannah the picture Thomasina drew of Septimus with the tortoise. It proves that the hermit was Septimus. Gus, in Regency fancy dress, is almost like a ghost from the nineteenth century. He bows to Hannah and they join Septimus and Thomasina dancing round the stage.

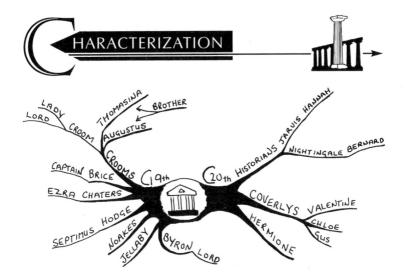

The Mini Mind Map above summarizes the main characters in *Arcadia*. When you have read this section, look at the full Mind Map on p. 31, then make a copy of the Mini Mind Map and try to add to it from memory.

The nineteenth century

Thomasina Coverly

In a stage note at the end of scene 1, Stoppard describes Thomasina as *an uncomplicated girl*. She is also, we come to realize, a child genius, who sees immense scientific and mathematical discoveries almost casually. The fact that she does not bother to write down the proofs she intuitively understands is the cause of Septimus's supposed madness in his two decades as a hermit, when he tries, without success, to re-establish them.

During the course of the play she ages from 13 to the eve of her 17th birthday: from uncomplicated girl to young woman who wants to learn to waltz, and to have Septimus come to her bedroom. But she never grows out of her excitement and her enthusiasm for what life has to offer. That bubbling optimism adds poignancy to the tragedy of her terrible death.

 Some students may be shocked by Thomasina wanting Septimus to come to her bedroom. But as sexual attraction has been spinning round the house for all the years she has been growing up, and as the relationship between her and her tutor appears to be both close and almost one between equals, it is not really so surprising. Thomasina is hungry for life, and she has learnt, unconsciously perhaps, from the adults around her that sexual attraction and secret liaisons are part of life. Her request for Septimus to come to her bedroom links to the beginning of the play when he, after making his 'embracing a side of beef' joke, tells her the facts of sexual activity in a way that is staggeringly blunt and honest

for the times. Prophetically, on being told the bare mechanics of sex (page 3), Thomasina says, *Now when I am grown to practise it myself I shall never do so without thinking of you.*

Thomasina never settles on one thing for long, but that is probably the result of the sort of education Septimus has given her. In their discussions when they are alone in the school room, they freely range from one area of study to another. They share an enormous common frame of intellectual and factual reference: the classics, art, the sciences, and so on. Thomasina's quick mind is not lacking the ability to focus; there is just so much for her to know and enjoy that she is always off seeking new knowledge and ideas.

❂ What impression do you gain of Thomasina's intellectual skills and interests as you read *Arcadia*? Remember she 'grows' from 13 to almost 17 during the course of the play.

In some ways Thomasina is quite isolated within the household, at least until her brother Augustus comes home from boarding school. She appears to know unconsciously that she is brighter than both her parents. We do not see any real relationship between Thomasina and her mother, who is always too busy being witty, worrying about the garden, or pursuing male guests. It seems unlikely that the daughter will share her father's *devotion to the sporting gun.* Brice and the Chaters she regards with a not-unkind condescension. It is hardly surprising that Septimus, the person with whom she spends so much time and who is closest to her in intellectual ability and interests, should become the man with whom she wishes to lose her virginity.

Septimus Hodge

Although he is one of the main characters in the play, there are many basic things about Septimus that we never discover. His closest companion throughout is Thomasina, but as we watch her grow up we learn far more about her as a complete person, her hopes for the future, her emotional inner life and so on. Septimus usually keeps his emotions hidden behind a screen of ironic wit. He seems exactly the same person at the end of the play as he was three years ago at the beginning.

Then, we are never really sure what he feels for the 13-year-old girl that he must refer to as *My Lady*. He could do this in an ironic and manner, or he could really resent having to be in such a position of subservience to the Crooms. When he teaches her to waltz at the end of the play, we are still not entirely sure of his feelings towards Thomasina: are they affectionate, loyal, lustful? He does kiss her *in earnest,* but he also seems quite adamant that he will not go to her room. Whatever else he may be, Septimus is a master of the coolly maintained appearance.

As tutor to the (we presume only) daughter of a titled and immensely wealthy family, Septimus is *not quite a guest but rather more than a steward* (Hannah, page 24). We also learn from Hannah that Septimus got the post by writing a letter of *self-recommendation.* This suggests that Septimus is not afraid to put himself forward when necessary, and perhaps also that the Crooms were not too bothered about who educated their daughter. Septimus has been to a good public school and Cambridge University, but in an age when servants without references from employers or sponsors could be out of work for years, Septimus was clearly taking a risk in writing his own reference.

But Septimus actually takes risks throughout the play. Remember, he could be sacked at any moment. He does not appear to have any private money of his own (on page 92 Thomasina finds him reading in the school room at night to save on candles). He seduces the wife of a guest, and he steers the conversation between himself and Lady Croom towards his risky declaration of passion for her in scene 5. Many of the things he teaches Thomasina, and his sometimes apparent indifference to teaching her at all, would have been unacceptable in even the most liberal households of the time. For a paid servant, he is certainly getting away with a lot at Sidley Park!

Of the nineteenth-century characters, he is the only one who does not appear to have ambitions or plans. Lady Croom wants to be Byron's and Count Zelinsky's lover, Noakes wants to build his picturesque garden, Brice wants his command to the Indies and Charity Chater as his mistress, Ezra

Chater wants renown as a poet, and Thomasina wants everything, especially to learn the waltz. Septimus must know his time at Sidley Park is drawing to a close as Thomasina becomes a woman, but we never hear him speak of what the future might hold for him. Of course, the tragedy for him is that he never leaves Sidley Park.

As with other figures in the play, it is difficult to make a realistic assessment of Septimus's full character for two reasons. First, he is living in a society so wildly different from our own that it is hard to imagine the restrictions imposed by daily life within the rigid social structure of a household like Sidley Park. Second, Stoppard is not setting out (in either of the play's timescales) to write naturalistic dialogue or create realistic, fully rounded characters. *Arcadia* is a highly stylized piece of writing, in which constant wit, irony and banter replace in-depth, fully believable characterization. It is also a play about ideas as much as characters. And in many ways, the witty, ironic, risk-taking tutor is the least realistic character of them all. This does not mean, however, that the figure Stoppard creates in Septimus is not entirely perfect for the role he must perform in the play's tragedy.

Ezra Chater

Chater is perhaps the most out-and-out comic character in the play. Stoppard cleverly never lets us hear a word of his verse, so we can only imagine just how dreadful it must be. Or is it? Like poor Thomasina, Chater dies (relatively) young, and the literary world has always been a back-biting gossipy one. Maybe Chater is actually quite good. Bernard has read 'The Couch of Eros' and says, neutrally, that it is *quite surprising* (page 21). An actor could invest these two words with all sorts of meaning: a facial expression of distaste, suggesting that he is being ironic and that the book is awful; or he could say it with sincerity, suggesting that Bernard has been pleasantly surprised by the quality of Chater's writing. Maybe Septimus and the others just attack his work for the fun of it. This is rather unlikely though: it is much easier to believe that, as in everything else we see about him, Chater the poet is a hopeless clown. But we don't actually know this.

Chater is vain, self-deluding, cowardly (he does not want to fight a duel, which is probably reasonable as well as cowardly!) and happy to live off other people who are in a better social or financial position than himself. And he has a wife who appears to drive other men crazy. We don't know if she is beautiful, or simply available, but she must have something about her that attracts lovers. We wonder what attracted her to Chater: he does not have a private fortune or a sparkling personality.

Nevertheless, you should remember that we hear more about Chater from other people than we actually see of him in person. Septimus is having an affair with Chater's wife, and might therefore look critically at Chater both as a man and a poet. Brice might push Chater towards a duel with Septimus which he knows Chater is likely to lose, so that he can marry Chater's widow. Lady Croom can be scornful of Chater partly because his wife got to Byron's room first. And remember that in the eighteenth and nineteenth centuries it was common practice for artists to seek wealthy and titled patrons who would keep them as extended guests at their great houses in return for a dedication in the artist's next book, or for a portrait.

The one thing that does make Chater indisputably and irrevocably foolish is his attitude towards his wife. He appears completely blind to her affairs. Then, more comically, he is fooled by Septimus into excusing her infidelities with the tutor. Even here it is just possible that Chater is trying to save face within the strict honour-bound society in which he finds himself as a guest at Sidley Park. Can he, as guest of Lady Croom's brother, really *call out* and maybe kill the family tutor? Perhaps he is being torn apart by rage and grief. But it is probably a fairer assessment to say that Stoppard has, in Ezra Chater, created another of those stock comic figures: the self-deluding man with a promiscuous wife who can run rings round him.

Lady Croom

Imperious, domineering, viciously funny, self-centred, relatively young and usually played as a beautiful and powerful woman: Lady Croom is all of these. She contributes more consistently to the humour of the nineteenth-century time-scale than any other character.

The only real emotion she ever appears to reveal is for her beloved garden. She may develop a curiosity, then a passion, for Septimus, but we never see a hint of any affection. Neither does she display more than wit towards her own daughter. The rest of the household she treats as *her troops* (page 13). Lord Croom is as distant and as rarely regarded by his wife as the horizon.

But Lady Croom is astute enough to know that she has power only over a realm she has created within a wider world completely dominated by men. Although she humiliates Noakes and despises what he proposes to do to her garden, in the end her husband will have the last word: the picturesque garden, hermitage and all, is eventually constructed. She also presumably knows that her affairs (or attempted affairs) can be carried out mainly because her seemingly dim-witted husband is more interested in shooting birds than having a loving and fulfilling marriage. Even an extremely moderate feminist reading of Lady Croom's position would conclude that she has created an empire to rule only through the indifference of men who could bring the whole thing crashing down if they chose. The 'reputation' of a great lady such as her could be destroyed by rumours. She could be giving Septimus power over her by allowing him to become her lover, however briefly their relationship actually lasted. Presumably she does not think it likely that her husband will trouble himself to find out, or that he would be too bothered if he did.

Despite her constant sarcasm, wit and irony-edged banter, Lady Croom does have a gentler, less abrasive side. She is passionate about the beauty of the garden, the 'Arcadia' of the title. She appears to have complete control over its day-to-day management, if not its long-term future. The artistic or philosophical notion of Arcadia implies a rural paradise of innocent pleasures. While most of the pleasure that is taken in the garden seems far from innocent, there is a sense throughout the play that a fragile, artificial paradise exists beyond the upstage windows. It is most eloquently described by Lady Croom (page 12). She may be regarded as the guardian of the garden, and the guardian (though certainly not the **personification**) of the spirit of Arcadia.

Richard Noakes

Noakes does not exist as a complete character. He is always seen in his professional role as a landscape gardener. He is also always out of his depth! But Noakes is important because he destroys the garden, the Arcadia, by his clumsy actions. Lady Croom loves the vision of paradise that she sees in her landscaped park, but Lord Croom allows Noakes to pull it all up in order to build a new garden in the 'picturesque style'. What Lady Croom ends up with is a mess! (For more detail on the artistic concept of Arcadia see the 'Themes' section of this guide.)

Despite the fact that he is cast as *middle-aged*, one might imagine Noakes as a gardener with a less than sparkling career. He appears to lack confidence, although his ideas are well laid out and conform to current fashionable tastes. He is often played on stage as though he is physically deferential to Lady Croom to the point of fear. It is easy to imagine that this is his great chance to play with 500 acres and a major commission that could make his reputation.

Like Chater, he is slow to pick up on the subtext of conversations going on around him. There are many places where Stoppard notes that he is *baffled* (twice on page 87 alone!). What we never really know is whether he is any good at his job. When Lady Croom gives her account of the destruction he has wrought (page 85), it may be simply that her dislike of what he proposes makes her condemn what is still work in progress. None of the twentieth-century characters ever comment upon the state of the garden that Noakes finally built.

Noakes destroys the Arcadia that Lady Croom loves, just as Capability Brown has destroyed the earlier garden from *the age of reason* that Hannah grieves for on page 27. But it is hard to see Noakes' actions as more than sad. He is too comic, too lightweight, to do anything evil. We can't make a case for him symbolizing the sweeping away of the old order, of the landscape of 'time never to be regained'. The worst that can probably be said of Noakes is that (if we are to believe Lady Croom's account of the garden alterations) he is messy and incompetent.

Captain Brice

A minor character, entirely motivated by his lust for Charity Chater, whom, after the death of Ezra Chater, he marries. He probably only offers to act as Ezra Chater's second for the duel in the hope that the poet will get himself killed, leaving Charity a widow.

He is yet another man at Sidley Park who is no match for Thomasina's intellect or Lady Croom's wit. Brice does not realize the irony in his observation to Septimus, *As her tutor, you have a duty to keep her in ignorance* (page 11), but Lady Croom is quick to score a point off him in the following line. She is in no doubt that her brother is somewhat slow-witted.

1809 At the beginning of the nineteenth century, the Royal *2000* Navy, in which Brice is a captain, might have been regarded in popular patriotic myth as the 'senior service', with 'hearts of oak', but the reality was rather different. So few ordinary men wanted to join it that press gangs roamed the coast, literally kidnapping men and forcing them to become sailors. Captains usually bought their commissions, and naval officers were not generally regarded as either educated or professionally gifted. What they lacked in brains they made up for with bluster and swagger. Captain Brice is Stoppard's version of this stock character type.

Augustus Coverly

A minor figure who has two roles in the play. His rudeness to Septimus, and then his admitted ignorance of the facts of life (which his slightly older sister has learned two years before Septimus puts him straight on the walk to dinner) show him in stark contrast to Thomasina. Augustus has had the expensive education at public school, but it is his sister who appears so much more intelligent, gifted and poised.

1809 Secondly, Augustus is the 'ghost' for the unspeaking Gus. *2000* On stage it is important that Stoppard's direction at Gus's appearance in Regency costume on page 96, *It takes a moment to realize that he is not Lord Augustus*, creates a striking and magical impression. It is in these dark, closing moments of the play that the leap between the two times is made in a magical way. Usually Gus and Augustus are played by the same actor to make this illusion easier.

Augustus/Gus: the two characters have the same name. Stoppard is not of course saying that time travel or reincarnation actually happens, just that the past is not always sealed off entirely from the present.

Jellaby

There are no poor people in either time-frame of the play. The Crooms and Coverlys are titled, wealthy and privileged. Hannah and Bernard are professionals with appropriate salaries, as presumably is Noakes. Septimus may be only a tutor, but he is very far from being a beggar. Jellaby is the only character who may come from an economically deprived background. However much he may have successfully cultivated an air of haughty detachment, he is still a servant, albeit the most powerful one in the great house.

Like Noakes, Jellaby never appears outside of his professional role, so we can safely say that for our reading of the play he is simply a butler. He conveys messages and, with some bribery, gossip (start of scene 6). The slightly bored manner in which he does this is a stock character trait that many writers have given to butlers – as if it is beneath the dignity of the role of liveried servant to take money for gossip, but 'well, one must do what is requested of one'.

In writing such a 'standard-fit' character, Stoppard is not being lazy, but having a joke about the conventions of stage-writing. Jellaby is a very minor character, and it is amusing to see him portrayed as the stock supercilious butler, more distant and haughty than the masters and mistresses he serves.

The twentieth century

Hannah Jarvis

 Chaps sometimes wanted to marry me and I don't know a worse bargain. Available sex against not being allowed to fart in bed (page 63). Hannah's outburst against Bernard's rather perfunctory suggestion that they have an affair, reveals a great deal about the woman behind the carefully maintained professional façade. The word *chaps* is hopelessly outdated, even among the sort of 'county set' that we don't really think Hannah fits into anyway. The reference to farting also reveals the streak of surprising crudity (she threatens to kick Bernard *in the balls* in scene 2) that we see her employ, rather artificially, as a shock tactic.

At her first (unspeaking) appearance on page 15, Stoppard notes that Hannah *wears nothing frivolous.* Although a spirited and independent single woman in her late thirties, it is easy to imagine something of the dry academic about Hannah. She won't dress up in costume for the party, nor be photographed. When she appears *dressed for the party, the difference is not however dramatic* (page 92). These stage notes suggest that Hannah should be played as a woman for whom fun and pleasure do not come naturally. She can be witty, and sparkle in an intellectual debate, but she is short on social drive and frivolity. One wonders if she is happy with this role that her character appears to have cast for her. She is surrounded by Bernard's seduction of Chloe, and Hermione's pursuit of Bernard, and is slowly unravelling the affairs that caused so much upset to the nineteenth-century characters. But *the attraction that Newton left out,* has left Hannah on the sidelines. There is no hard evidence to suggest whether Hannah is relieved or a little sad about this.

Despite the quote that opened this section on Hannah, there is somehow a hint about her that she would like to let herself go a little more. Perhaps this is why she bows to Gus (or to the spirit of the vanished age) and dances. There is a wistful symbolism in the directions for the closing wordless moments of the play that have Septimus and Thomasina, the dangerously illicit couple, dancing *fluently*, while Hannah and Gus keep *a decorous distance* and dance rather awkwardly. Perhaps Hannah longs to be *fluent* like Thomasina.

Other people notice Hannah's inability to express much emotion. Although the play proves that her caution and logic mean she will succeed academically where Bernard has failed, Bernard is probably right when he says, *It takes a romantic to make a heroine out of Caroline Lamb. You were cut out for Byron* (page 63). Back in scene 2 Hannah has expressed a longing to see the gardens dating from the *age of reason* that were destroyed in *the decline from thinking to feeling*. (The barb in Bernard's observation is that Byron is regarded as one of the foremost writers of the Romantic Movement.)

In other ways, however, Hannah is more of a risk-taker than Bernard. He has a salaried post at a university, while Hannah makes her living purely from freelance writing. And she appears to have a real feel for the era and the characters she is researching, to want to connect with them in some emotional way. Bernard appears to see his research more as a means to further his career.

1809 / 2000 Feminist critics could define the differences in professional approach between Hannah and Bernard in gender terms, but any attempt at a simplistic 'Hannah does it in a female way, Bernard in a male', is doomed to failure. For there are (professionally at least) too many overlapping common elements. Bernard accuses Hannah of lacking confidence in her own professional intuitions (*By which I mean a visceral belief in yourself*, page 50), but Hannah later claims she has exactly that feeling about the portrait on the cover of her Caroline Lamb book that Bernard says is the wrong picture. Bernard talks about just having to look hard enough for the proof to find it, and Hannah, who remains at Sidley Park quietly working while Bernard rushes about then storms off to London, is finally rewarded with the proof of the hermit's identity. It is not really helpful to draw a simple gender-based distinction between Bernard and Hannah – the characterization is too subtle.

Bernard Nightingale

Although Hannah and Bernard share a professional style of debate, if she is the quiet one, he is the noisy tear-about. This even affects the way they use humour. Hannah is much more subtle and cutting in her put-downs, Bernard relies more on the full-frontal insult (*No you fucking idiot, we're talking about Lord Byron the chartered accountant*, to Valentine, his host, page 50). ❂ Make two lists, noting the main differences (and any similarities) between Bernard and Hannah.

Bernard is more of a larger-than-life character than Hannah. Some elements of his personality are pure comic exaggeration. It is unlikely that he would steam-roller his way into Sidley Park so easily (even if both Chloe and her mother are attracted to him). He might have to be a little more deferential to Valentine. But Bernard's role is to drive the plot forward and to create confusion. Even his first appearance causes upset, first by his using a false name, then by the accidental revelation of his real identity. The positive side to all this energy is that Bernard drives the theme of decoding history (or making it up if the evidence doesn't fit or is hard to find!) through the first two-thirds of the play. He constantly reminds us that *Arcadia* is, to a large extent, a play about history, and that history can be exciting!

Bernard is plainly and unashamedly motivated by professional ambition and personal lust. He never wavers in their pursuit. In both areas he enjoys brief successes, but utter confusion by the end of the play. It is interesting to note that he has left a tearful Chloe and a furious Hermione, has been *fucked by a dahlia*, and departed in a dishevelled state like a character in a farce, before the poignant 'time-jumping' silence of the final all-revealing moments of the play. Maybe Bernard just makes too much noise to hear the truth he has struggled to uncover.

But Bernard is not entirely without genuine feeling and passion. He tells Hannah how, when with Chloe, he *spotted something between her legs that made me think of you*; then, after being slapped, he gives Hannah some vital information for her research. So Bernard does keep to his side of the academic bargain. Despite deliberately engineering an obvious sexual confusion here, Bernard wants to be seen as the cool professional academic when it suits him.

Sadly, he uses the reading of his lecture, and the subsequent debate, as not merely a platform to put over his beliefs about what happened at Sidley Park in April 1809, but as an attack on everyone else – Valentine especially – whom he thinks is not taking his lecture seriously. This shows Bernard to have both a big ego (which we could have fairly assumed for some time) and a tendency to become personally involved in academic disputes which professionals should keep as just that: academic. The argument, which spans pages 59–65, becomes unpleasant and *ugly*, and this is largely down to Bernard pushing it that way, as Stoppard notes at the top of page 60.

Although we might sympathize with Bernard's no doubt genuine and impassioned claim for the ascendancy of the artistic experience (his big speech at the bottom of page 61), he does turn the 'arts v. science' debate into a nasty attack on the mild-mannered Valentine. Bernard here is no 'knockabout' comic character; such humour as there may be in his lines is cutting.

Stoppard seeds just a few suggestions about something that could fuel the anger, principally from Bernard towards Valentine, but also, to a lesser extent, the other way. Bernard could dislike Valentine for the class that the Coverlys represent. There is nothing obvious in how Stoppard has written Bernard to suggest what sort of social background he is from. Sussex was (at least at the time the play was written in 1993) one of the more politically radical universities.

On page 23, Bernard refers to Valentine as *Brideshead Regurgitated*. This is a reference to Evelyn Waugh's famous novel *Brideshead Revisited*, about a hugely rich and privileged family who own a colossal country estate. On page 64, Bernard says, *This is my first experience of the landed aristocracy. I tell you, I'm boggle-eyed.* And when Valentine reappears after Bernard has effectively driven him from the room after their dispute in scene 5, Valentine says of him, with cutting dismissiveness, *I don't care to be rubbished by the dustbin man.* Perhaps the two men have a mutual dislike for one another based on class prejudice.

Valentine Coverly

The oldest of the Coverly children, home from studying mathematics at postgraduate level at Oxford. The fact that Valentine is at Oxford, the oldest university in the world, could add to Bernard's dislike of him: maybe Bernard would really like to teach there.

Valentine has a certain oddness about him that we can see in Chloe and perhaps sense in Gus. (Although Gus never speaks, he brings Hannah an apple and later bows *a regency bow* to her before they dance.) Stoppard hints throughout that the Coverlys may be quite a strange crew, the classic over-bred, upper-class family locked in their private world at Sidley Park. But Valentine is out in the real world in so far as he is studying at Oxford, something you don't get to do (at postgraduate level anyway!) just because you're a member of the landed gentry.

Valentine is rather a gentle, wistful soul. He has a pet tortoise and appears to have been working away on his family game books, using them as raw data for mathematical experimentation, for some time. What we don't know is how long he has known Hannah. This is presumably only so long as she has been working at Sidley Park, but we don't know how long that has been. They do seem very comfortable in one another's company, though the greatest passion to which their relationship rises seems to be good friendship. The none too well developed joke (all on Valentine's side we assume) of Hannah being engaged to him is rather odd. Maybe Valentine is such a shy and retiring fellow out in the big world, that he has latched quite seriously onto Hannah, whom he conveniently finds living under his own roof. But he is cast about ten years younger than her, and there seems to be no real passion even hinted at between them, so it appears that the engagement is a kind of whimsical fancy that amuses him, and that Hannah goes along with it. Their most explicit banter around sex is on page 75, where they quickly settle to working quietly on their separate researches at opposite ends of the table. It is interesting to speculate that this might be the sort of relationship that Hannah would really opt for.

Chloe Coverly

Chloe is not deliberately written in a way to demean the character, or type of character, she is by virtue of birth, but neither is she a figure who controls anything much in the development of the plot. Her main function is to be seduced by Bernard, who is around twenty years older than her.

She does not appear to be an innocent girl just out of school who gets fooled by an older man. She has set her sights on him by the end of scene 2. Chloe is a little rich girl who knows what she wants. Though she is reduced to tears when Bernard flees at the end, we get the feeling they are mostly from shock, and for show. She will be fine in the morning. Maybe she is going to develop into a modern-day Lady Croom, or another version of Hermione, her mother, who has also been making advances to Bernard.

One thing appears certain from the small part Stoppard has written for her, she is not going to represent a reinvented, modern-day version of Thomasina, like the Augustus/Gus pairing. Chloe is pretty lightweight intellectually.

Gus Coverly

No one explains why Gus never speaks, though we can see that he is socially delicate. He hates people shouting. Bernard (or Stoppard through the character of Bernard) could be making a dig at the inbreeding for which the landed classes are humorously, if not deservedly, famous.

On the other hand, Gus is a quiet and gentle presence to offset the upsets that Bernard (principally) causes in the modern-day time-frame of the play. His silence, and his convincing transformation into Regency dress at the end of the play, create a magic that links the two eras.

The unseen characters

It is important just to mention the influence of the various unseen characters that hover about the edge of the plot. And if you didn't buy (or read) the programme at a stage production, you might be waiting all evening for one of them to show up! They are important to the way the plot develops.

The nineteenth century

Mrs Chater

Mrs Chater is charming and spirited, with a pleasing voice and a dainty step … – and yet her chief renown is for a readiness that keeps her in a state of tropical humidity as would grow orchids in her drawers in January (page 7). Never has a character that we never see on stage been given such a rousing introduction.

We are left to imagine her as a mixture of nineteenth-century sex kitten and charming society woman. She certainly has the power to drive men wild. She is also saddled with a boring, vain husband, and we wonder why she married him.

Lord Croom

Obsessed with shooting and nothing much else, Lord Croom may simply be blind to what his wife does, or maybe he just doesn't care. The few details Stoppard gives of him suggest another in that line of (real and fictional) dim-witted country gentlemen of plain and unrefined appetites. He doesn't appear to accompany Lady Croom to London when she sees Byron at the Royal Academy. He certainly doesn't share her love of the garden at Sidley Park (as it stands in 1809), and we don't really believe he is having it remodelled because he is a fan of the new picturesque style. More likely he is just following fashion.

Lord Byron

 We bring to *Arcadia* our own knowledge of the real Byron. Stoppard assumes we know that he was one of the three great poets of the Romantic Movement (along with Keats and Shelley). He was also the one who enjoyed most fame as an individual, though to the romantic image of the hell-raiser, rule-breaker and freedom-fighter one must add the persistent rumour that he had a more than brotherly interest in his half-sister Augusta Leigh!

Polite society of 1809 would have found Byron daringly dangerous to know. Women adored him, but men – other than fellow Romantic artists – found his political and philosophical passions and unconventionality disquieting. But he did have a title, so Lord Croom probably feels comfortable about having Byron on his shooting party.

For more information on Byron, see page 4 in the 'Context and Background' section of this guide.

The twentieth century

Lord and Lady Coverly

Hermione fancies Bernard and apparently makes no bones about it. She spends her days researching her garden. Lord Coverly hates Japanese cars, won't answer typewritten letters and has a problem with gays. A typical reactionary but an essentially harmless caricature of the English landed classes then! That's what Stoppard wants us to think, and he creates a perfectly acceptable background figure to hover unseen about the play. The current Lord is as uninterested in the research going on (and the affairs or potential affairs of the women of the house) as Lord Croom is about his wife's passions.

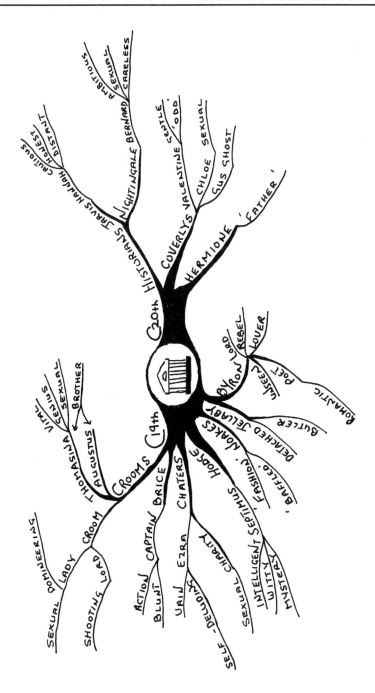

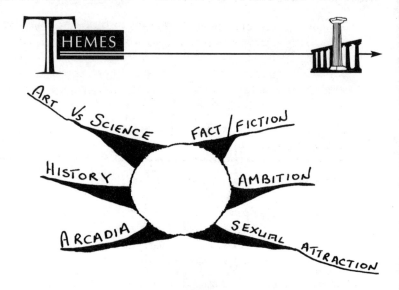

ART VS SCIENCE   FACT / FICTION

HISTORY   AMBITION

ARCADIA   SEXUAL ATTRACTION

A **theme** is an idea which runs through a work and which is explored and developed along the way. The Mini Mind Map above shows the main themes of *Arcadia*. Test yourself by copying it and then trying to add to it before comparing your results with the version on page 38.

Fact and fiction

The interpretation of historical evidence is one of the main themes in the play. It animates both Hannah and Bernard, though they have different motives and are trying to find out 'what really happened' in different ways. They are searching for facts, but Bernard ends up creating a fiction. One of the key ideas in the play is how we can know that historical 'facts' really are facts at all.

Thomasina is also looking for facts, in the form of mathematical and scientific proofs. Remember, she was living and studying in an age when scientific knowledge was far less fixed and proven than it is today. In 1809 many of the basic laws on which we found our understanding of the world were either not formulated or were yet to be proved true.

Thomasina's grasp of iterated algorithms is 150 years ahead of them being accepted and used as a mathematical technique. Her insight into the second law of thermodynamics pre-dates the final formulation of the law by about forty years. She is a brilliant child looking for facts in a world where many theories held to be true by adults are in fact fictions.

Ambition

Ambition is the spring that drives many of the characters – and Bernard most obviously so. He does not merely want to consolidate his academic reputation, he wants the glory of fame. One of the play's key messages might be that Bernard is *fucked by a dahlia* because he wants fame too badly. He does not stop to check his sources.

Hannah is also ambitious, but in a different way to Bernard. While he seems excited by the things he uncovers (he is a bit like a tabloid journalist, but his stories are nearly 200 years old!), Hannah seems genuinely moved by what she finds. Bernard sees the characters he is working with as a means to make a name for himself: Hannah seems to connect and feel for them on a much more human level.

Valentine may have professional ambitions like Bernard and Hannah, but he is much more low-key about them. He works away quietly, and is upset when he has to give up his mathematical research into the family game figures because there is too much *noise*, too many extraneous factors affecting the figures.

Chater is talentless and ambitious. He does not talk about what rewards his new book might bring him, but he sees his presence as a guest at a great house as the result of his writing his first collection of verse. (Of course we know it is because Brice, who is infatuated with Chaters's wife, is the brother of Lady Croom.)

We do not know if Septimus has ambitions to rise above his position as a paid tutor, and if he sees the best way of doing this is to get into Lady Croom's bed. Septimus never reveals much of himself, and we do not know what his feelings (beyond, presumably, lust) for Lady Croom might be. He never talks about how he sees the future after Thomasina reaches the age of 17 and his services are no longer required.

Thomasina of course is the brightest of all the characters, a budding genius. But she is too swept up with looking forward to the pleasures life will bring her to even think about ambition. She is young and wealthy, and probably in love with her tutor. She is the one character who could probably achieve her ambitions effortlessly, but she doesn't bother to think about them. In a sense she rises (however briefly) above all the others as they search for success in their various ways.

Sexual attraction

The attraction which Newton left out is a force that wreaks havoc among a cast of characters who, on the surface, appear to have a great deal of self-control and detachment. Notice that no one appears to be looking for a committed and loving relationship. They are in lust, not love. Most of the sexual liaisons break social rules, and none seems likely to last beyond a few nights of passion. Sexual attraction in *Arcadia* does not appear to lead to lasting happiness. But as no one mentions the word 'love' with any seriousness, perhaps no one is actually disappointed. Ezra Chater might be the only candidate for someone seriously hurt by the constantly changing sexual network, but he is apparently too self-absorbed and vain to notice what his wife gets up to. As for the never-seen male 'lords of the manor' (Lord Croom, and Coverly Snr), they aren't even in the picture! Whatever they know or suspect of their wives' sexual interests never enters the play.

The list of sexual pairings in the play involves most of the characters:

- Septimus has 'a fling' with Charity Chater. He also has sex with Lady Croom, at her instigation, though it is suggested that this might have developed into a longer-term affair for some of the time-lapse between 1809 and 1812.
- Brice has either already had, or will have, an affair with Charity Chater.
- Charity has a fling with Byron.

- Lady Croom is infatuated with Byron and Count Zelinsky.
- Bernard seduces Chloe, but is also pursued by her mother, Hermione.
- Valentine claims to be, or to want to be, Hannah's fiancé, though there never appears to be more than an easy companionship between them.

Arcadia

The *Oxford Companion to English Literature* (1946 edition) defines the idea of Arcadia as 'an ideal region of rustic contentment'. It is an aesthetic idea, a sort of innocent country society. Many poets of the Romantic Movement wrote poems about this imaginary place (often featuring nymphs and shepherds!), and painters produced landscapes depicting its rural charms.

Many landscape gardens were designed and built to capture this ideal. It is an artistic not a naturalistic concept, and this is reflected in the landscapes that the garden designers created: beautiful but artifical lakes with mock classical temples nestling in groves of specially planted trees.

The play's title refers literally to the landscape outside the windows at the back of the stage set. But it also refers to another less literal idea. The Latin phrase misquoted by Lady Croom *Et in Arcadia ego* is often confused with another phrase *Et ego in Arcadia*: 'I too have lived in Arcady.' This is usually used in a broader sense to refer to a time of joy or happiness that has now vanished. (See also Commentary, p. 56.)

A key theme of the play is the inevitable tragedy of lost time and lost happiness: what one critic called the 'heartache for time never to be regained'. We might assume that Septimus is happy with his life, up to the point when Thomasina accidentally kills herself. He then spends the rest of his life trying to prove what she so effortlessly saw. He dwindles to a miserable hermit, presumably tormented by grief for the girl who died and the time they spent together.

Bernard and Hannah do not actually say what they think about the era they are both studying, but we can assume from many of the things they say about elements of it that they do, on some level, look back to a time that might have been a sort of Golden Age. Bernard is thrilled by the idea of Byron and his contemporaries living in the house where he is now researching. His impassioned speech on page 61, where he quotes Byron, suggests more than a cold academic interest in the time when the poet was alive. Hannah's speech on page 27 is a passionate appeal for the original, long-destroyed garden at Sidley Park: again, it is far more emotive than an academic researcher needs to be. Bernard and Hannah both look back to a vanished era with some longing.

History

The study of history is the main activity of two of the modern-day characters, and a key theme of the play. Septimus and Thomasina also discuss history (page 38, the burning of the library at Alexandria). *Arcadia* is a play both about history and partly set in a historical period. This theme links closely with that of 'Fact and fiction'. Historical truth and interpretation are discussed in more detail there (see p. 32).

Valentine is keenly aware of the history that surrounds him at Sidley Park. He describes the game books as *my true inheritance* (page 46).

The staging of the play suggests the idea of history existing like an after-image in the present. The room in which Bernard and Hannah work is the same room where the events they are trying to trace actually occurred or are talked about by the participants. The final scene blends characters long-dead with those still living. The play's ending visually suggests that history is still, in some ghostly way, alive in the present.

Art versus science

A debate that has run for years and years! People have long argued over whether science and scientific knowledge is more important than the arts and creative expression. Stoppard does not use *Arcadia* overtly to contribute his own ideas to the debate, but the dispute between Bernard and Valentine in scene 5 does run out a few key ideas on either side of the debate. In that scene, the dispute breaks up because Bernard becomes too aggressive in his arguing with Valentine. But equally, no side 'wins' because Stoppard gives both characters an even-handed set of valid reasons. It is impossible to speculate on Stoppard's personal view of the 'arts v. science' debate, but from the way he has written these characters, it would appear he quite sensibly comes down on neither side. They see them as different things. Scientific knowledge is enlightening and essential to our understanding of the universe in which we live; artistic experience feeds something in our emotions and our souls.

When writing about *Arcadia* for exam or coursework purposes, try not to get bogged down in the wider implications of this debate. Concentrate on what the characters say about it, especially in scene 5.

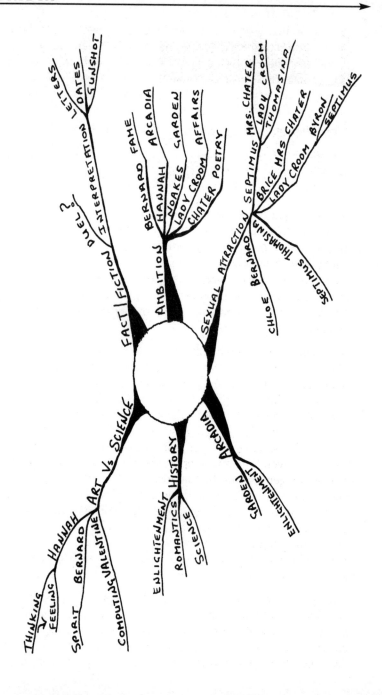

Language – explaining 'big ideas'

Arcadia is written in two distinct styles: 'early nineteenth-century' speech and contemporary language. In fact, the nineteenth-century dialogue of Septimus, Thomasina and the rest may be more of a pastiche or approximation of how people actually spoke in the early 1800s than an accurate representation, but the effect is perfect for the generally light and bantering style of that part of the story. This style also contrasts with the dialogue of Hannah, Bernard and the other contemporary voices. Notice that, for example Bernard and Hannah swear at one another on more than one occasion. This would be unacceptable to any of the nineteenth-century characters.

Both parts of the story involve characters explaining big ideas. Thomasina gropes towards refuting Newtonian determinism, understanding the second law of thermodynamics and developing the mathematical notion of iteration – all before her 17th birthday! But her explanations have all the suddenness and fly-by-night ease of a child's way of describing their thoughts. Sadly, in Thomasina's case it slowly becomes clear that given time and support she could have flowered into a scientific genius. But the 'big ideas' she so lightly expounds glide effortlessly into the dialogue of the play. We hardly realize that we are watching or reading a scene in which people are discussing something as abstruse as Newtonian determinism until we, as it were, step back and think about it. Stoppard makes this subject-matter almost as easy to interpret as, say, the plot of a mystery or a love story.

Among the twentieth-century characters, Hannah, Valentine and Bernard all have 'big ideas' to explain. Their accounts, perhaps because they are about things closer to our own culture and experience, or because they use language like our own, tend to be points where the focus of the play opens out from the events that are happening within it. Thus, Bernard's impassioned speech about the need for knowledge to be self-knowledge if it is to be meaningful (pages 61–2) is one of the moments when this most self-serving and narrowly focused character speaks with genuine feeling about things that exist beyond the confines of the immediate drama. He is putting forward one side of a debate that is often heard in contemporary Western culture: the value of artistic experience versus that of scientific knowledge.

Like their nineteenth-century counterparts, Hannah, Valentine and Bernard tend to explain complex ideas in clear and relatively non-technical language. This helps us understand the crucial but complex intellectual basis for the play. Hannah and Bernard both use images and comparisons to make the ideas they are struggling to convey easier to understand. Bernard should be able to do this: he is a professional university teacher. Hannah appears proud of the fact that she does not teach, but she is a best-selling academic author so is presumably used to having to make complex theories understandable. Valentine is less skilled at explaining mathematical theories, but then he not a professional communicator. Like the other twentieth-century Coverlys, he is not a naturally eloquent speaker, and he is also beginning to despair of his involvement with complex mathematical theory. Nonetheless, his long speech on pages 47–8 is a mixture of mathematical information and excitement about the opportunity to make new discoveries.

Hannah is in some ways the most eloquent of the twentieth-century 'thinkers', probably because in addition to being naturally cautious she is the most modest, yet quietly thorough and assured, of the three. Her only outburst of mixed intellectual explanation and emotion is in the beautifully constructed speech at the bottom of page 27. Here she both shows her despair for the changes made to the gardens at Sidley Park and compares these changes to the decline from *thinking to feeling*, from the Age of Enlightenment to the Romantic Era. It is a marvellous blending of exposition and feeling, and perhaps tells us more about Hannah's character than any other speech she makes.

❂ What do you think Hannah is revealing about her personality in this speech? Does she reveal these facets of herself anywhere else in the play?

If there is one key difference (style aside) between the speech of the nineteenth-century 'thinking' characters and the twentieth-century ones, it is that the former deal with intellectual ideas more lightly, more apparently effortlessly, than the serious professional twentieth-century writers and students. Look at Septimus's long speech on pages 37–8. He presents a huge philosophical picture of the world, of the march of time and the acquisition of all knowledge. Nevertheless it flows lightly, and seems to be almost as much an attempt to console Thomasina, who is dismayed by the loss of the books burnt in the library at Alexandria, as a stating of a great philosophical position. It ends with the introduction to a practical joke.

❂ Imagine if Bernard had been given this speech, and that Hannah (for example) had been expressing the same despair as Thomasina. How do you think Bernard would have expressed himself? How would his tone have compared with Septimus's light and optimistic one?

These key speeches where the play's big ideas are expressed contrast with the otherwise quite light and often humorous dialogue that flows between the characters in both parts of the plot. The explanation of ideas interrupts the comedy of much of the rest of the play. See the 'Humour' section (p. 43) for details of how Stoppard uses language to comic effect.

Structure

Arcadia is a two-act play, telling two complementary stories set in different periods. These stories begin by being staged in separate scenes, but interweave more and more closely towards the end of the play, when characters from both stories share the stage. Stoppard has used this 'split time' device in other plays. In *Indian Ink* he also employs the device of contemporary researchers trying to piece together the past. In *The Triumph of Love* the poet and classicist A. E. Houseman, the play's main character, is played by two actors. One depicts him as recently dead, going across the mythical River Lethe into the afterlife. But this river also becomes the Isis in Oxford, and along it, in a punt or on the bank, comes the young and very much alive Houseman.

Stoppard is a master of the play that operates in two distinct periods. In *Arcadia* the props make the journey from the nineteenth to the twentieth century. In the second act characters from each century coexist on stage, though they do not ever 'time travel' and acknowledge each other. There is, however, a sort of coming together at the very end, when stage directions suggest that when Gus appears in nineteenth-century costume we should at first be uncertain whether it is actually him or Lord Augustus, Thomasina's brother. And the play ends movingly with the two couples, one from the past, one in the present, waltzing together round the stage. It is surely this wordless finale that adds to the tragic power of the play. We know that perhaps within minutes of Thomasina's first waltz ending she will be burnt to death.

For a play that is so full of words, of complex discourse and explanation of difficult ideas, *Arcadia* has very strong and vital physical directions, and uses non-verbal effects at key moments in the development of the plot. Apart from the end of a play, the main climax usually occurs just before the interval. In a thriller, for example, some revelation can be made which sends the audience off for an interval drink discussing what this new information might lead to in the second half. But in *Arcadia*, the first Act ends with a shift back from twentieth to nineteenth century, to an empty stage where all that happens is an off-stage pistol shot. On the page it might appear that the Act rather peters out, but we are aware of the significance of the shot out in the garden. At this stage we believe it is the duel. It leaves us wondering who, if anyone, has been shot. This is the question we bring back to the second Act.

For more details of how the two stories can coexist on the same stage, see the 'Staging *Arcadia*' notes at the end of this section.

Humour

There is a great deal of humour in *Arcadia*. Characters are often far more comic than they would be if the play were attempting straightforward realism. There are also many more comic situations and misunderstandings than is strictly believable or likely. Most of the time the characters employ humour intentionally, such as Lady Croom's almost constant ironic sarcasm. Other humorous elements are created by situations and not intentionally by the characters. For example, the initially unexplained appearance of the twentieth-century characters in Regency dress creates a humorous effect that is only later explained by the costumed dance.

Stoppard uses humour to help the audience through what is a complex play about difficult ideas. He does this so cleverly that the comic and serious elements of the text do not jar but support one another. He is an enormously skilled and experienced stage writer and he knows the expectations that a contemporary audience bring to the theatre. They may want a play that will make them think deeply about complex ideas, but they also want to be entertained. (Striking a balance between an intellectual experience and a 'good night out' has always been a key issue for playwrights – think about how many Shakespeare plays have comic subplots for light relief.)

In reality, none of the characters would spend as much time making jokes as they actually do in the play. A nineteenth-century aristocratic family like the Crooms would be unlikely to make so many quips to their tutor as Lady Croom engages in, and Septimus would be far more deferential to his titled employers. Even in the more liberated twentieth century, two academics are unlikely to develop comic banter so quickly after meeting for the first time. And the various situations, seen on stage or reported to have occurred in the garden, which give rise to comic misinterpretation and confusion, are more akin to modern farce than real life, and to the confusions that arise in Shakespeare comedies such as *Twelfth Night* due to misunderstandings. Stoppard skilfully manipulates the type and level of humour throughout the play to entertain the audience, but never allows it to overwhelm the seriousness of the ideas explored nor take away from the terrible tragedy of Thomasina's death.

Stoppard employs a whole battery of comic techniques. Many characters in actual eighteenth- and early nineteenth-century plays were written to display their ability (and that of their creators) to be witty. Often this involved complex and lengthy word-play and quick, cutting replies or ripostes. It was duelling with words instead of swords. Stoppard develops this style of comic writing, bringing in other types of humour more common in the modern world. He seamlessly blends contemporary humour with a style of comic writing that was at its peak 200 years ago. ❂ What key differences are there between the comic language and style of the humour engaged in by each set of characters – between the nineteenth-century and contemporary voices in the play?

Below is a list of the main comic devices Stoppard uses, with definitions and an example of each from the play.

IRONY

Definition. Characters are engaging in irony when they say something but really mean the opposite of what their words apparently express. This device is normally used to be sarcastic or to ridicule the person being addressed. One of the commonest ways of using irony is to seem to praise a person or thing, when a moment's reflection reveals the apparent praise to be carefully worded criticism or insult. Irony occurs all through the play.

Example. Lady Croom, talking to Septimus about Ezra Chater's willingness to be deceived by his wife, says (he) *finds proof of his wife's virtue in his eagerness to defend it.*

SARCASM

Definition. Sarcasm is simply any bitter or cutting remark that is not just a blunt insult, but there is an enormous range from plain 'put downs' to cunningly worded attacks. Lady Croom (again!) is an expert in sophisticated and biting sarcasm. She variously attacks almost every other character in the play. She is very much the mistress and ruler of the world in which all the eighteenth-century characters live. They depend on her literally for food and shelter. She is the most powerful figure in the play. We never see her husband, who is probably truly the lord and master, though Lady Croom may have the cutting sarcasm necessary to rule him as fully as she does the others in her household.

Example. Lady Croom reserves particular sarcastic venom for Noakes and his plans for her garden. On page 12 she ends a cutting catalogue of disapproval of the changes Noakes plans with a comment about *a fallen obelisk* that he is hoping to errct (or let fall!) in place of her current Chinese bridge. Noakes tries to defend his plan by saying, *Lord Little has one very similar*, to which Lady Croom bitterly but wittily replies, *I cannot relieve Lord Little's misfortune by adding to my own.*

It is worth remembering that Lady Croom is a relatively young and attractive woman, not a bitter old dame passing out cutting remarks with the supposed wisdom of age. She is younger than Noakes, and only ten years older than the tutor to her daughter. The fact that she is a lively and attractive woman adds to the power of her criticisms. And being literally the lady of the house with power over men who otherwise would be living in a society where they (by virtue simply of gender) would be in a superior position to most women, adds a real twist to her attacks.

WORD-PLAY

Definition. Using either the potential for double meaning in words or phrases, or substituting words with similar-sounding ones, to create a comic effect. This is generally a more gentle form of humour than irony and sarcasm.

Examples. The first example of word-play occurs in the opening lines of the play when Septimus deflects Thomasina's potentially tricky question about the meaning of *carnal embrace* by punning on the words *carnal* (sexual) and *carne* (Latin for 'meat'). So he manages, for a short while at least, to convince Thomasina that a *carnal embrace* involves not sexuality but *the practice of throwing one's arms around a side of beef.*

Lady Croom has some gems of word-play that are much more cutting, echoing the power of her use of irony. On page 83 she refers to Noakes, who with Lord Croom's permission is tearing up and none too successfully rebuilding the garden, as *'Culpability' Noakes*. The word-play here is against the nickname of the most famous and gifted English landscape gardener of all time, 'Capability' Brown, already mentioned by Hannah as having designed the version of Sidley Park that Noakes is destroying.

MISUNDERSTANDING

Definition. There are countless examples of characters misunderstanding one another with comic results, or deliberately misunderstanding what is said to them as a way of creating irony or engaging in sarcasm.

Example. An example of genuine and extended misunderstanding that creates comic confusion occurs at the bottom of page 9 and through page 10 when Lady Croom is listing the features of her garden that Noakes wishes to demolish. While Noakes and Lady Croom understand they are speaking of garden plans, Chater and Septimus believe she is referring to the incident where Septimus made love to Charity Chater in the gazebo. Septimus further believes he has been spotted at other places in the garden where he has met Charity and tries to defend the claims. It is left to Thomasina, as ever more quick-witted than those around her, to put Septimus right.

ABSURDITY

Definition. Absurd humour turns on an idea or situation being so out of the expected, of things being so out of usual harmony, that the result is comic.

Example. There are several important examples of absurd humour in the play. Bernard's lengthy academic research 'proving' that Byron fought a duel at Sidley Park, killed Chater then fled the country is demolished by a reference in Lady Croom's garden books to dwarf dahlias. That so much academic work can be destroyed by something so simple and trivial as a plant is absurd, leading to Bernard's comic heartfelt outburst *Fucked by a dahlia!*, and later to Hannah's vicious little dig at Bernard's distress *Think of it as a breakthrough in dahlia studies* (a truly ironic line).

WIT

Not perhaps quite as easily definable as other types of humour. The ability to demonstrate a quick and cunning wit was an essential requirement of men and women in upper-class eighteenth- and early nineteenth-century society. In *Arcadia* it is obviously the characters in the nineteenth-century part of the play who use the more wit. A witty remark should delight and amuse with its mixture of brilliance and surprise. It is a lightweight type of comedy, though if it is loaded with venom then it can be very closely associated with irony and sarcasm.

Example. Lady Croom's observation on duels fought by men over women, page 72, *Indeed, I never knew a woman worth the duel, or the other way about.*

VISUAL HUMOUR

This is obviously not so easy to pick up on when reading the play, but the stage directions do give some strong pointers to things that would appear humorous in a production.

Examples. On page 67 Jellaby, the supercilious and aloof Butler, takes the dead rabbit from Septimus *without enthusiasm.* Imagine this acted on stage, the immaculate and very superior Jellaby making a show of lifting the carcass with obvious disdain and distaste.

Another important example of visual humour is contained in Chater's reaction when he spots the flaw in Brice's comment at the bottom of page 42. All Chater actually says is *Oh! But … .* However, this indicates that he has just realized that for Brice to kill Septimus, as he has just promised, they would have to fight a duel together, but as it has just been arranged that Septimus will first fight Chater, Brice will get his shot at Septimus only once Chater himself is dead! The actor playing Chater has to invest a lot of visual humour in that simple *Oh! But …* to bring the scene to the comic finale it requires.

Staging Arcadia

As you read *Arcadia* notice how thorough and detailed the stage directions are, and how carefully Stoppard lists the things that gradually accumulate on the table: especially the books, primers and notes that appear at various points.

It is a convention of writing for theatre that a playwright lists in the stage directions only those props which are essential to the play. Some published plays do contain very detailed accounts of the layout of the set and even the lighting, but this is usually a description of a particular production, usually the first one. Such details have been added to the script after the production. As a general rule, actors work with a script that contains only general descriptions of the set to help them plan out moves, entrances and exits and so on, plus a list of essential props and where they are 'set' (located).

Arcadia has only one set. There are no scene changes. This rather bare room is set with a relatively small but wide-ranging collection of props that gradually increases during the play. We never see the park, the Arcadia of the title.

Try to imagine these props as they accumulate on the table. Try to visualize those that can be 'handed down' from the nineteenth to the twentieth century: the portfolios, the geometrical solids, the tortoise (Plautus and Lightning could be the same animal, as tortoises live a long time!). Keeping these key props in your mind's eye will help you with the details of the complex plot as you read the play. Stoppard has included nothing in his highly specified props list which is not vital to the plot.

The most complex of all the props, and the ones that Stoppard is at greatest pains to keep track of, are the notes, drawings and books that are produced and read by the nineteenth-century characters and searched for by the twentieth-century ones. These are the crucial physical links between the two ages. A simple note scribbled quickly by Charity Chater becomes a significant but misinterpreted research find for Bernard. Thomasina's mischievous addition of a hermit to Noake's drawing of the garden becomes a significant piece of evidence in Hannah's quest for the identity of the 'Sidley Park Hermit'.

❂ Find other examples of documents changing their importance from the nineteenth to the twentieth centuries, or of documents being misinterpreted by the researchers.

The putting of notes into books, the lending or inscribing of books and the burning of other letters are all part of the plot, sometimes crucial to the mechanics of it, sometimes just important to tie up loose ends. Try to follow the significance of all the stage directions that Stoppard gives for the various books and notes. Each time you come across one, try to understand exactly why the direction is given. For example, on page 14, scene 1 ends with the direction that *Septimus opens Mrs Chater's note … folds it and inserts it into the pages of 'The Couch of Eros'*. We later realize why this is important. Lady Croom insists that Septimus lends Byron his copy of Chater's 'Couch of Eros'. Septimus does not have time to remove the note, so when it is discovered in the twentieth century Bernard leaps to the conclusion that it was Byron's book and that Charity Chater's note was to the poet, not to Septimus.

❂ What is the significance of the drawing which Gus hands Hannah at the end of the play? How exactly will it help her research?

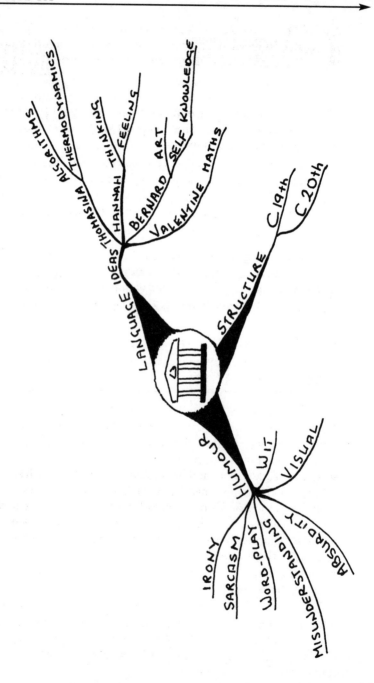

The whole play takes place in one room. The *Arcadia* of the title is a huge landscape garden beyond the French windows 'up stage' (at the back of the set).

The play is in two acts. When performed there is an interval between them, at pages 52–3. Unlike Shakespeare plays, where the scene numbering starts fresh at the beginning of each new act (Act 1 scene 1, Act 2 scene 1, and so on), in *Arcadia* the scenes are numbered straight through from 1 to 7.

The long last scene is the only one where characters from both time periods are on stage simultaneously. Stoppard describes this as *doubled in time*. Although they may be standing side by side, characters from different eras cannot see or hear each other.

Act 1

Scene 1 – 1809

◆ Septimus discusses sex with his pupil Thomasina.
◆ Ezra Chater challenges the tutor to a duel. Septimus has been having an affair with Chater's wife. Septimus charms Chater by praising his poetry.
◆ Noakes, Lady Croom and her brother Edward Brice arrive. Chater and Septimus mistakenly think that Lady Croom's objection to Noakes's plans for Sidley Park is a reference to the tutor's making love with Charity Chater all over the gardens.
◆ Noakes plans to remake the park in the *picturesque style*. Lady Croom is unimpressed.
◆ Thomasina draws a hermit into Noakes' picture of the garden he is planning.

The play opens with a joke. This sets the tone for much of the dialogue throughout the play: fast, witty and clever. It is worth looking in detail at this opening joke (bottom of page 1) as it is a good example of how Stoppard uses language to comic effect.

Thomasina has overheard the phrase *carnal embrace* and wants to know what it means. This is an old-fashioned (but not in 1809) expression for having sex. Septimus deflects her enquiry by making a pun on carnal and *carnis*, Latin for flesh or meat, such as a shoulder of mutton. Then there is word-play within the joke: *a haunch of venison well hugged* turns on the fact that venison (deer meat) is supposed to be 'hung', left to rot very slightly, before it can be eaten. An *embrace of grouse* is word-play on the fact that grouse are traditionally sold in pairs called 'a brace.' As you can see, Stoppard's jokes are not simple one-liners. You have to read this play very carefully!

The relationship between Septimus and the 13-year-old Thomasina is light-hearted. She feels free to chat to her tutor about anything that comes into her head. He has set her to find a proof for Fermat's last theorem, a famously impossible mathematical problem. This will keep her quiet while he reads Ezra Chater's new book of poetry. Septimus might appear not to be taking his responsibilities as a private tutor seriously, yet he does answer all Thomasina's questions.

From the very start of the play, Septimus and Thomasina appear to be the cleverest of the 1809 characters, and the most intimate. They seem easy in each other's company, although Septimus is a paid tutor, not much more than a servant to the Crooms.

Thomasina is a lively and intelligent girl. ✪ How much of this do you think is down to Septimus's 'unusual' way of educating her? How much is she a naturally gifted child? What clues might Stoppard be giving us in the opening few pages of the play to help us decide?

Thomasina tells Septimus how Mrs Chater was *discovered in carnal embrace* with someone in the garden. Now half the servants know. Eventually Septimus tells Thomasina what carnal embrace really means. His wit and irony are maintained during this simple 'sex education lesson': when Thomasina asks if *sexual congress* is the same as love, he replies (near the top of page 4) *Oh no, it is much nicer than that.*

Thomasina's lively mind never sticks on one thing for long. After a brief interruption from Jellaby the butler, she forgets all about sex education and is wondering why the jam in a rice pudding *will not come together again* once it has been stirred! This leads the easy-going lesson into philosophical discussion about free will. On page 5 Thomasina shows that she is quick to latch onto ideas that are new to her, and not afraid to question them. They begin to discuss Newtonian physics, which in 1809 was a cutting-edge scientific theory about the nature of life and matter.

Ezra Chater's arrival brings their discussion to an abrupt halt. Stoppard is careful throughout the play to balance intellectual discussions with action and events of a more human nature. Many of the characters have a long speech at some point where they explain their particular interest or belief. But the action always moves swiftly on.

Ezra Chater arrives in a temper, for it was Septimus who was having sex with Mrs Chater in the *gazebo* (summer house). Septimus is prudent enough to get Thomasina out of the room before trying to deal with this wronged husband. Septimus and Chater are both guests of the Crooms and bound to a code of polite behaviour. Chater is a friend of Captain Brice, Lady Croom's brother: Septimus is a hired tutor. But Septimus feels able to challenge Chater and, finally, to win him over. Of the two men Septimus is much the cleverer. Chater is easily fooled and terribly vain.

Chater claims that Septimus has *insulted* his wife by making love to her. Septimus turns this into a joke by saying that he would have insulted her if he had not turned up, and he will not be slandered by anyone suggesting that he failed to appear. The joke lets Chater know that his wife sent a note arranging the meeting, though Chater does not seem to pick this up. He appears convinced that his wife is virtuous. When he says to Septimus *I am calling you out*, he is using an expression, like 'demanding satisfaction', that was traditional when issuing a challenge to duel.

We don't know at this stage whether Septimus is afraid of duelling or if he is just playing with Chater, but at the bottom of page 6 he begins to manoeuvre the argument to avoid a duel. At the top of page 7 he makes a pun on the word 'satisfaction'. ❂ What two meanings of the word create the pun? What does Septimus's joking reveal about his attitude to Chater?

He then insults Mrs Chater in a most detailed way, involving her sexual *readiness* (and notice he uses the word *renown*, suggesting she enjoys a certain fame for her sexual activities), and her reputation which *could not be adequately defended with a platoon of musketry deployed by rota*. In other words, Septimus is using the most comic and imaginative language to tell Chater, 'Your wife is famous for her sexual affairs.' But Stoppard, through Septimus, puts it so much better than this!

To anyone with more awareness and less vanity than Chater, this could trigger the duel instantly. But the only thing Chater has actually heard is the almost passing remark Septimus has made about not wishing to shoot a poet *of the first rank* dead in a duel. Septimus is slyly feeding Chater's ego. The latter seems not even to have heard Septimus's attack on Mrs Chater's reputation, and with a couple of prompts is happily off discussing the qualities of Milton and Southey. The implication is that Chater dares to think himself equal to these great poets. By the bottom of page 7 Chater is won over.

Danger looms when Chater says he *would very much like to know the name of the scoundrel who slandered my verse drama 'The Maid of Turkey' in the Piccadilly Recreation*. It was in fact Septimus writing anonymously. But again Septimus runs rings round the slow-witted Chater. The only time Chater seems to pick up on what Septimus is saying is when (on page 8) he notices that Septimus does not say it is his *estimation* that Chater's new book will *take the town*, but that it will be his *intent*. Chater grasps that Septimus is saying he will be writing a review of it.

Chater has a great talent for self-deception. As Septimus describes the long process of preparing to review the book, Chater convinces himself that his wife knew Septimus was writing a review so had sex with him to make him look on her husband's poetry more generously. By the bottom of page 8 Chater is delighted with what his wife has done. ❂ Why does Septimus seems momentarily thrown by the reference to Captain Brice at the top of page 10?

Septimus has so entirely won Chater over that the poet insists on inscribing Septimus's copy of his book. The choice of words is unfortunate! At this point Mr Noakes, the landscape (or *landskip*, to use the early nineteenth-century spelling) gardener arrives ✪ Why does Noakes *panic* when he sees who is in the room? Why is he *rooted* to the spot by Chater reading the inscription aloud?

Noakes has been employed, more by Lord than Lady Croom it appears, to remodel their 500 acres of gardens. (This is equivalent to two or three good-sized modern farms.) Lady Croom delights in the garden as it is, a traditional country park laid out by the most famous landscape gardener in English history, 'Capability' Brown. Noakes's design is in the new *picturesque* style. The garden is full of winding streams, classical temples and groves of trees. Noakes plans to construct fake ruins in a mock wilderness.

Lady Croom must burst onto the stage at the bottom of page 10. She is written as the most powerful character in the play. Lord Croom may have control over her (he is after all happy to let Noakes remodel the garden even though Lady Croom likes it as it is), but we never meet him. Lady Croom rules over her guests.

There is an extended comic device based on confusion that runs through page 10 until Thomasina, as ever cleverer than anyone else around her, explodes it. Lady Croom and Brice are listing the features of the garden that Noakes wants to destroy: Septimus is convinced they are cataloguing the places where he has had sex with Mrs Chater.

Thomasina's mention of *carnal embrace* closes the joke. Her reference to the Italian painter Salvator Rosa (whom neither her mother nor her uncle have heard of) shows her to be probably brighter than any of the adults, except Septimus. ✪ What is Stoppard doing when he prefaces Noakes's line at the top of page 11 with the note *Answering the wrong question*?

Lady Croom and Brice are concerned that Septimus may have corrupted Thomasina with talk of sex. Thomasina's answers suggest that she is aware of what she is doing and is really playing with her mother and slow-witted uncle. When her mother turns to Noakes, it is almost as if she has given up trying to win any points off her daughter. Lady Croom's comment at the bottom of page 11, *Mr Noakes – now at last it is your turn*, shows just how in command Lady Croom sees herself to be. She has come into the school room and is dealing with everyone there in turn.

Lady Croom's first love is her garden. In two descriptive speeches (pages 11–12) she speaks with passion (mixed with the irony she can never resist) of the beauty of the garden as it is and the horrors of what Noakes is proposing to do to it. She is basing her comments on the drawings he has shown her that are described in a lengthy note back on page 10. (There, Stoppard refers to Humphrey Repton, another great landsape gardener who was famous for the way he showed 'before and after' views of gardens he was commissioned to rework.)

Lady Croom finishes the second of her 'garden speeches' on page 12 by mistranslating a famous Latin epigram that appears in paintings by Guercino (Italian artist, 1590–1666) and Poussin (French artist, 1594–1665). (It should read, 'Even in Arcadia, there am I.' In the paintings it is next to a skull or on a tombstone, referring to death.) When Thomasina challenges her, Lady Croom's judge-like attention turns on her daughter. Her comments, however (pages 12–13), are entirely flippant. After the passion she has just expressed for her garden, this suggests that she might think more of the landscape than of her daughter! But with Lady Croom you never know how she really feels, and the mother–daughter relationship between her and Thomasina is not important to the plot of the play.

Again showing her total command of the group gathered in the school room, Lady Croom accuses Noakes of having got ideas about the garden from reading too many 'Gothic' novels. When Chater corrects her over the authorship of a book, she says that while Chater is her guest the novel *was written by whomsoever I say it was, otherwise what is the point of being a guest or having one*. In other words: 'I'm in charge and whatever I say is the case, even if you know it to be wrong.'

The scene has moved on through a series of interruptions and entrances. The final phase is begun by the sound of gunfire. The hunting-obsessed Lord Croom is getting closer to the house with a shooting party. Lady Croom concludes the idea of her being in command by referring to the guests who must follow her out as her *troops*.

Left alone, Thomasina and Septimus enjoy peace after all the argument and confusion of the scene. Septimus casually quotes the correct translation of the Latin epigram, and Thomasina immediately understands the connection with death. She playfully draws a hermit into the picture of the hermitage that Noakes has left behind to show what he hopes to build in the garden.

She gives Septimus a note from Mrs Chater. The fact that she has waited until the others have gone shows that she is not only academically gifted, but also quick to pick up on the affairs of adults. The scene ends with Septimus inserting the note into the book of Chater's poems that has just been inscribed by the author. ✪ Why will the inscription and the note in the book become so important later in the play?

Test yourself

- ? All of the characters have a long speech at some point where they explain their particular interest or belief. Find places in the play where the following characters do this: Septimus, Hannah, Bernard, Valentine.
- ? If you have read the whole play, how does Thomasina's remark (middle of page 6) about a note in the margin link to something much later in the play?
- ? Draw a Mini Mind Map of all the characters we have met so far, then add branches listing the main things we have learnt about them in this scene.

You can run out to play now like Thomasina if you wish. Or just take a break and prepare to meet the modern-day characters.

Scene 2 – Present day

- ◆ Bernard Nightingale comes to visit Hannah Jarvis. We meet Chloe and Valentine, daughter and son of the present Lord and Lady Coverly.
- ◆ Bernard conceals his identity as he wrote a very critical review of Hannah's last book.
- ◆ Bernard is researching Ezra Chater. He has a theory that Byron fought a duel with Chater at Sidley Park and killed him. But he lacks concrete evidence.
- ◆ Hannah is researching the *Sidley hermit* for a new book. No one knows the identity of the hermit.
- ◆ Bernard wants Hannah to co-operate with him. She is suspicious.
- ◆ They both demonstrate their knowledge of the areas they are researching.
- ◆ Chloe lets slip who Bernard really is. Hannah is furious.
- ◆ When Hannah tells Bernard that Septimus was probably a school friend of Byron's, Bernard is ecstatic. He decides to work alongside Hannah.

The change in period is sharply established in the first few lines. Imagine the change of mood in a theatre production. The way the modern characters speak creates this, as much as their clothes. Valentine's opening word, *Sod*, would not have been uttered by any of the nineteenth-century characters. But the school room remains completely unaltered. Read the lengthy notes that start this scene: they give information about the props that is vital to understanding how the plot works.

1809/ There is a lot of information conveyed in the conversation
2000 between Chloe and Bernard. We learn who Hannah is and what she is doing at Sidley Park. We learn that there is to be a garden party, *our annual dressing up and drunkenness* (top of page 17). We learn that Noakes must have got his way and rebuilt the garden, for Chloe says, referring to Hannah (page 16), *I bet she's in the hermitage.* But we don't know yet why Bernard doesn't want Chloe to give Hannah his real surname.

Bernard meets Valentine and the unspeaking Gus. Valentine is looking for the commode where the family's game books are kept. Stoppard is creating the impression of a rather eccentric aristocratic family (though Chloe seems normal!). ✪ What other things on pages 18 and 19 suggest a slightly odd family?

1809/2000 During the interlude when Bernard is waiting for Hannah, Stoppard provides some **backstory** (background information about the characters or plot, provided in dialogue). Hannah is writing about the garden and the hermit. Bernard is an academic from Sussex (University). Bernard's speech deriding an attempt to analyse a story on a computer (page 19) is an indication of things to come. Bernard does not believe that science and scientific method are as valid or as important to human experience as art.

Stoppard gives a note to Bernard's first line to Hannah, he *turns on the Nightingale bonhomie*. ✪ How is this immediately shown in Bernard's conversation, bottom page 19 over to 20? How does Hannah react?

Bernard likes the sound of his own voice and holds strong opinions. This almost ruins the effect of his 'charm' when he gives a far too gushing speech about *ha-has* (page 20). A ha-ha is a simple ditch device that does away with fences at the edge of big country gardens, but still keeps animals out. It gave a sense of the garden going on into the countryside without limits. Hannah is unimpressed by Bernard's enthusiasm and knowledge. The reference to *Murray* is to John Murray (publisher, 1745–93) who knew and published Byron, as well as travellers' guidebooks which would have mentioned landscape gardens and features such as ha-has.

1809/2000 From the bottom of page 20 and through page 21, Hannah becomes increasingly bored by, then infuriated with, Bernard's attempt to charm her. His praise of her last book leaves her cold and by the middle of page 21 she is putting on her shoes again *to kick you in the balls*. This rather uncharacteristic outburst prompts Bernard to explain the reason for his unannounced visit to Sidley Park. Although studying different things, Hannah and Bernard are interested in the same period of history and literature, and Bernard is the sort of man who sees everyone as a potential rival, so he is guarded about what he reveals.

Bernard fills in the few known details of Ezra Chater as a historical figure. Of course we have met Chater already. We have seen the human being behind the bare historical facts. Confusion between historical fact and modern interpretation – sometimes due to lack of information, sometimes to rash judgements – is a key theme of *Arcadia*. ❂ Bernard has already made one great error in his assessment of Chater (on page 22). What is it?

1809/ From page 22 to Hannah's key speech at the bottom page
2000 25, Bernard and Hannah engage in a conversational sparring. Information about their professional interests is revealed, as well as details of the Coverlys, the current titled owners of Sidley Park. We learn that Valentine is engaged in postgraduate biology studies. When Hannah speaks of the bad review she got from someone at Sussex University called Nightingale, Bernard doesn't flinch. Gradually he gets what he wants. Hannah shares some of the details of Sidley Park in 1809, especially what she has found out about Septimus. The tone of the conversation throughout these pages is light and combative. Stoppard is creating an exaggerated parody of the sort of knockabout but knowledge-laden arguing in which some academics love to engage. He turns a style of professional discourse into dry comic banter.

The mood is altered by Hannah's speech at the bottom of page 25. Here we feel she is speaking about something that she truly believes. She describes how the garden was rebuilt as fashions and appreciation of the arts changed from 1730 to 1809. The garden is used as a metaphor for *the decline from thinking to feeling*. She sounds as if she actually despairs that the great intellectual ideas of the Enlightenment were pushed aside by the Romantic Movement's focus on personal experience and emotion. This speech also tells us a lot about Hannah's personality, that she is more tuned in to thoughts and intellectual processes than emotions. It is a neat explanation of a great deal of art history and prepares us for her much more impassioned speech at the bottom of page 27, when she returns to the same ideas but expresses them with real feeling.

In between Hannah's two speeches, Bernard puts on a little show of his own academic skills with his interpretation of a letter in an 1860s *Cornhill* Magazine that Hannah shows him. Stoppard is really poking fun at the tendency of some academics to hoard their discoveries as children do favourite toys. Bernard is showing off by playing with one of Hannah's prize discoveries. A key fact which we need to remember from this part of the scene is that the Crooms 'kept' a hermit who lived in the hermitage that Noakes built for over twenty years. The hermitage was stuffed full of papers covered with unfathomable mathematics. Hannah sees the hermit as **personifying** the ruin caused to intellectual thought by the Romantic Movement's focus on feelings.

✪ Do you think Bernard is being sincere when he says *That's awfully good* at the top of page 28? What might be going through his mind?

Through pages 28–9, up to the arrival of Chloe, the two academics seem to draw closer together. There is a sense of shared professionalism. But when Chloe reveals Bernard's surname Hannah is furious. The patronizing review he gave her last book still pains her. Bernard shows himself to be a cunning 'game player' when, immediately after Chloe's slip has left him in an awful position with Hannah (and he needs her help remember; she's got to Sidley Park first!), he suggests that he and Hannah should collaborate. He knows Hannah would like to regain her standing among Byron scholars (her last book was on Caroline Lamb, who was infatuated with Byron).

1809 Bernard reveals his theory that Byron was at Sidley Park *2000* in April 1809. Using Septimus's copy of Chater's book of poems as evidence, he builds up a theory that Byron fled from England in 1809 because he killed Ezra Chater in a duel at Sidley Park. Of course, the snapshot we have been given, in scene 1, of Sidley Park back in the early nineteenth century hasn't yet given us anything to suggest that Bernard's theory is totally wrong. But he is already misinterpreting the note that he quotes on page 31, which we know is from Chater to Septimus, not Byron. Moreover, on pages 30–2 Bernard is clearly filling in a lot of gaps with imagination and speculation. Hannah is much more cautious and their arguing breaks out once again.

Then Hannah reveals wearily that her research into Septimus shows that he was at university and public school at roughly the same time as Byron. They could have been friends, and therefore Byron could have been visiting his old school pal at Sidley Park. This is only a possibility, but Bernard is ecstatic. He instantly believes that he now has a definite lead to link Byron with events at Sidley Park in 1809. His excitement seems genuine when (bottom of page 32) he kisses Hannah and decides to stay in the village to work alongside her. Notice that he doesn't ask permission from Hannah or the Coverlys. He is like a dog on the scent of his quarry: nothing will put him off.

Chloe's 'chatting' with Hannah about Bernard winds the long scene down to a calmer pitch as it reaches its conclusion. Chloe is not interested in what professional arrangement Hannah may have made with Bernard. She just wants to know if the older woman fancies Bernard – and if not then, well, Chloe seems ready to be in the running! We also learn that Valentine is claiming to be in love with Hannah. Hannah's flippancy does not give anything away about this. In fact, we never really know if Hannah and Valentine have any feelings for each other beyond friendship.

❏ When Hannah says *Oh dear* at the end of the scene, what is she worrying about? What is the possible symbolism of the apple as a gift?

Test yourself

❔ Make a Mind Map with two main branches, one for Hannah, one for Bernard. Add everything we know so far about their characters. Just how different are they?

❔ Make a list of sources of evidence (books, papers, letters) that Bernard and Hannah have between them by the end of this scene. (Keep the list: it will be useful later on!)

Don't decline from thinking to feeling tired. Take a break now before going back to the nineteenth century in the next scene.

The next two scenes return us to 1809, then back again to the twentieth century. They are shorter than the first two. Stoppard has introduced both time periods with their separate casts and now needs to keep the pace of the whole play going by not lingering too long in one time. After the interval, in Act 2, the drama of the developing plot will allow more time to stay in one era, but for now the bones of the complicated story are still being drawn in, so pace is the key.

Scene 3 – 1809

◆ We learn that Byron is Septimus's friend, and is staying at Sidley Park. Byron has let slip to Chater that Septimus wrote the attack on Chater's last book.

◆ Septimus is writing notes and letters while Thomasina translates a Latin text.

◆ Thomasina again shows her intelligence. She and Septimus appear more like friends than tutor and pupil.

◆ They discuss Cleopatra and the burning of the library at Alexandria. Septimus gives a speech on the nature of time and human achievement.

◆ Chater arrives with Brice to challenge Septimus to a duel.

◆ Lady Croom demands that Septimus lends Byron his copy of Chater's new book of poetry. Various notes remain tucked inside it.

◆ Septimus becomes angry and says he will fight Chater and Brice and kill them both.

Jellaby gives Septimus a letter. We don't learn who it is from until later in the scene. Thomasina is struggling to give a verbal translation of a Latin passage (the *unseen*) that Septimus has set her. Latin was a classical language that any well-educated person of the time was supposed to study. It is worth noting, however, that even aristocratic families like the Crooms often thought daughters not worth educating very much: just enough to make them witty and charming young brides! So the fact that they let (assuming they know!) Septimus teach Thomasina Latin, science and mathematics suggests they are an enlightened and free-thinking family. ❂ From what we see of Lady Croom and learn about her husband, do you think this is the case? Or is Septimus taking charge and planning Thomasina's education?

Septimus seems to be hardly paying attention to Thomasina until his pupil says how she saw Byron and her mother in the gazebo. The stage note says *Septimus's pen stops moving, he raises her eyes to her at last.* Thomasina has certainly grabbed his attention: he is no doubt remembering what he got up to in the same summer house! ❂ What might this reveal about Septimus's feelings for his employer, Lady Croom?

Thomasina tells how Byron let slip to everyone at breakfast, including Chater, that it was Septimus who wrote the bad review of Chater's book. Byron is either incredibly careless, or deliberately stirring up trouble for Septimus. Either way, Septimus, as so often, does not reveal his feelings about the problems he knows this will create.

The lesson spins on into a discussion of mathematics. Thomasina clearly has an insight into complex mathematical ideas, even if her knowledge of them is incomplete. On page 37, Thomasina gives a long speech in which she sketches out her theory for a mathematical basis for evolution. Septimus appears to pay little serious attention it. (Sadly for Thomasina and her tutor, Valentine will later reveal that the girl really was onto something quite astounding.) By the top of page 38, the lesson switches back to the Latin text, a description of Cleopatra in her barge. Thomasina is disdainful of the classical queen who was destroyed through love. Perhaps she is unconsciously drawing a parallel between Cleopatra and the adults at Sidley Park making fools of themselves through passion and love. (Historical note: the Alexandrian library was famous in ancient times for containing, it is said, four million manuscripts, many of which were accidentally burned when Julius Caesar was besieged in the Egyptian city.)

1809/2000 Thomasina shows her knowledge of history and classical texts when she mourns for the great works of ancient literature destroyed when the library was burned. Septimus's long speech on page 38 is one of several key points in the play where characters talk in depth about something they believe in. Septimus tells Thomasina that she should not grieve for the great works that were lost because everything will be invented anew at some time, now or in the future. Septimus's philosophical view is essentially optimistic: everything can be regained in time. ✪ Do you think the play proves him right or wrong?

After this long speech, the pace and tone of the play quickly shifts when Septimus plays a joke on Thomasina. He pretends to be offering a 'first sight' translation of the Latin he set her, but she quickly sees that it is a piece of work he has already studied and translated. She runs out in a rage, passing Brice and Chater who are on their way into the schoolroom.

Septimus knows why they have come. The letter he did not answer was from Chater. Brice, a naval captain and perhaps keen to be seen as a man of action, is eager to confront Septimus but Chater hangs back. The poet is not spoiling for a fight, even though he knows Septimus has seduced his wife and made fun of his book. ✪ Look back to scene 1 and find exactly what Septimus said about it.

Chater is acting as if Brice is his second (supporter) in a duel. He asks that Septimus speak not directly to him, but to Brice. Chater could be grateful for this means to avoid an open quarrel, but Septimus turns it into a farce (top of page 40). But when Brice seems insistent that a duel will be fought, Septimus gives up the game. ✪ What reason could Brice have of his own for wanting Chater to fight a duel? What outcome might Brice be hoping for? (Look to the top of page 9. What is inferred?)

Byron's being present and Septimus's friend is mentioned yet again. This is the fourth mention of the famous poet in this scene, no doubt to underline his unseen presence to those in the audience not quite up to speed with what's going on! ✪ Check back and find the previous three.

Chater seems keen to avoid having to fight a duel in which he might be killed. But before either a challenge can be made or an apology accepted, Lady Croom enters. She wants a copy of Chater's new book for Byron, with whom we might suspect she is infatuated. She takes Septimus's. It still contains the three notes that Septimus put in it. He is aware of this and obviously would like to get them out, but you don't argue with Lady Croom!

1809/ *2000* So the book that will end up with Byron and be found by Bernard nearly two centuries later now has in it:

1. Ezra Chater's note from scene 1 accusing Septimus of seducing his wife.
2. Charity Chater's note.
3. Chater's second note delivered by Jellaby at the start of this scene.

The fact that these are found in a book left in Byron's library will lead Bernard to assume that they were addressed to Byron, even though the book is inscribed to Septimus. None of the notes mention Septimus by name.

Lady Croom dominates the situation in the school room. When Chater protests that Byron only wants a copy of his new book to make fun of it in a satirical review, she replies, *Well of course he does Mr Chater. Would you rather be thought not worth insulting?* This is a shrewd observation, reflecting the world these characters inhabit.

Lady Croom may have personal reasons for not wanting Byron to undertake his plan to travel to Europe. She is being established as a woman attracted to men, despite her haughty demeanour and endless irony. She demands that Septimus take Byron's pistols from him. She thus provides two pieces of information that Bernard will never know: Byron was already planning a foreign trip and did not flee after killing Chater, and the pistols that might have been used in a duel were not in Byron's possession when the duel was supposed to have taken place.

Brice seizes on the mention of pistols as Lady Croom exits. This time Septimus rises to the challenge and says bluntly how he will *answer* Chater, *By killing him. I am tired of him.* Septimus has finally lost his temper. When he says that after she is a widow Mrs Chater *will not want for protection while Captain Brice has a guinea in his pocket*, he is suggesting that Brice has already seduced her, or wishes to do so, just as he (Septimus) has already done. When Brice reacts furiously, Septimus agrees to fight him as well, after he has fought Chater. We don't know if Septimus is a confident and skilled duellist or is just angry, but this last page of the scene shows him in a completely new mood, one which never resurfaces in the remainder of the play. ❷ What is the *flaw* that makes Chater exclaim *Oh! But ...* at the end of the scene?

Test yourself

❓ Re-read Septimus's long speech on page 38. Try to encapsulate his view of life and culture in a single statement.

❓ Although we never see Byron, his presence is vital to the plot. Make a Mini Mind Map of what we know about him, or what people think of him, from what is said in this scene.

❓ From the evidence in this scene only, describe Septimus's attitude towards Thomasina.

Scene 4 – Present day

◆ Hannah and Valentine (a mathematics research student) discuss the *iterated algorithm* she has found in Thomasina's lesson book.

◆ Valentine is doing maths research using data from the estate games books.

◆ Hannah believes that Thomasina might have been an unrecognized child prodigy.

◆ Valentine says it is impossible for Thomasina to have made the discovery.

◆ Bernard has found a note that he believes proves Byron (not Septimus) seduced Chater's wife. Bernard thinks this will make his reputation.

◆ Hannah says Bernard's evidence is too slight.

1809/2000 Notice the complex notes for what books are on the table. The notes, and the books in which they are put and later found, are very important. They provide vital evidence that both Hannah and Bernard are trying to find, and which Bernard misinterprets. Misreading of history is one of the themes of the play: how can we be certain that things we believe happened actually did occur? Is our interpretation of historical events and evidence always hit and miss?

The first part of the scene, up to Bernards's arrival on page 49, does two things:

- establishes the relationship, almost entirely intellectual, between Hannah and Valentine;
- through Valentine's talk of mathematics, explains the idea that Thomasina had about *iterated algorithms.*

Hannah is asking for Valentine's help in understanding Thomasina's note in her textbook. Notice the link back to Septimus's telling Thomasina in scene 1 how the mathematician Fermat wrote a note in a book saying he had a proof for his famous theorem, but did not have space to write it there in the margin. This started a search for a proof that kept mathematicians busy for centuries.

Stoppard is faced with a difficult task. He has to make complex ideas understandable to an audience sitting in a theatre, most of whom are quite naturally more interested in how the relationships between the characters will develop. But *Arcadia* is based as much on ideas as on characters, because it is ideas and the quest for knowledge that drive most of characters. ✪ Make two lists: (1) characters who are basically pursuing ideas and knowledge, and (2) those who are pursuing other characters! (The lists are not mutually exclusive!)

From the bottom of page 43 to the bottom of 48, Valentine basically holds court, answering Hannah's questions. Up to now he has been presented more as one of the household than as an intellectual in his own right, with ideas and knowledge central to the plot. Look at the number of lines Valentine has on these pages compared to Hannah. But he is responding to Hannah questions, and Hannah is a good listener.

He explains that Thomasina was working on an idea that would show *the mathematics of the natural world.* Her idea was to use the results of one equation as the starting point for a new one, over and over again, *like you'd blow up a detail of a photograph, and then a detail of the detail and so on, forever.* She was using the results to plot a graph which would show the form or shape of an object. At this stage none of the contemporary characters know exactly what her big plan was. They only have the evidence of her maths primer, which is full of equations but far too few for any conclusion to be reached.

Valentine links iteration to the work he is doing using the raw data of the estate game books. This is maths of the highest order, numbers being used to explain natural events such as population growths and long-term weather patterns. Maths like this could reveal the structures and hidden patterns of the natural world. But as Valentine says, the theory has only been around for about twenty years. He believes that, in the end, *She was just playing with numbers. The truth is, she wasn't doing anything.*

❂ Compare Valentine's explanations in this scene to Bernard talking about the possible Byron scandal in scene 2. How does each man present their ideas, and what do these different approaches reveal about their characters? If Hannah had been asking Bernard for information from his chosen field of interest, how do you think Bernard would have responded?

Valentine's long speech on pages 47–8 is his key moment to explain what excites and drives him in his professional research. Although he starts with the possible outcome of what Thomasina might have been trying to do, he widens the focus to talk about the challenge of cutting-edge mathematics used to explain natural phenomena. Imagine it acted on stage. Maths is not usually an emotionally charged subject! But we can imagine Valentine becoming more and more enthused with his subject, until he concludes, *It's the best possible time to be alive, when almost everything you thought you knew is wrong.*

His high emotional pitch is quickly brought back to earth with the arrival of Bernard, who is working in the house, *going through the library like a bloodhound.*
❂ What does this phrase suggest about Bernard's approach to his academic research?

Bernard has found a copy of 'English Bards and Scotch Reviewers', a satirical poem written by Byron in which he attacked many other poets of his day. Lady Croom has already said (page 40) that Byron intends a second edition, and wants to borrow Septimus's copy of Chater's book so that he can read it and include a review.

❂ Byron really did produce 'English Bards and Scotch Reviewers' in 1809, but of course with no mention of

Stoppard's fictional Ezra Chater! What is the effect of Stoppard blending historical fact and fiction here?

1809/ 2000 Bernard is convinced that the note jokily deriding Chater's book 'The Couch of Eros' is in Byron's hand. ☉ Could it be? He is even more excited when Hannah give him a letter she has found in which the wedding of Brice to Mrs Chater in 1810 is mentioned. Bernard is in a passion of excitement, but Hannah is far more cautious. This difference between the way they approach their researches is crucial to the rest of the play. Hannah reminds Bernard that he hasn't actually proved that Byron was ever at Sidley Park. So Bernard becomes positively ecstatic when Valentine almost casually drops the fact that Byron is listed in the game book for 1809. Read the stage notes at the top of page 51, and imagine how Bernard will appear on stage when the Byron connection is revealed to him.

After a brief joke about Lady Coverly *being in a flutter* about Bernard (which pairs nicely with the other lady of the house, Lady Croom, being infatuated with Byron nearly two hundred years earlier), Hannah and Valentine return to discussing Thomasina's mathematics. After Bernard's frantic excitement, their final discussion creates an air of calm at the end of the scene. Valentine admits Thomasina could have done the maths, but that she would have needed a computer to get enough equations into the process to arrive at an answer. His last line is rather chilling: he doesn't believe she did the maths, because *you'd have to be insane.* ☉ What do you make of this comment?

Test yourself

? Look through the scene carefully. Note any places where simple emotions (affection, anger, etc.) are clearly expressed by one character for another. What does this suggest about the people who we meet in this scene?

? In a few lines, explain what Bernard now believes happened between Byron and both the Chaters in 1809 and 1810.

? How does Valentine's remark that ends the scene link to the 'Sidley Park hermit'?

In a stage production this would be interval time. Have one yourself, but avoid the gin and tonics. Ask yourself, what will happen next?

Act 2

Scene 5 – Present day

◆ Bernard reads his lecture to Valentine, Chloe, Gus and Hannah.
◆ Hannah says Bernard's evidence is still dangerously incomplete.
◆ Chloe defends Bernard, who has seduced her.
◆ Bernard attacks Hannah's latest book.
◆ Valentine and Bernard argue about art and science. Chloe and Valentine leave upset.
◆ Hannah and Bernard continue to debate, Bernard now slightly more friendly. Hannah rejects his offer of sex. He leaves for London to give his lecture.
◆ Valentine and Hannah discuss the Sidley Park hermit. Hannah is staying to look for clues to his identity. Two documents suggest he may have been Septimus.

Stoppard's comic focus in this scene is to satirize the vanity of academics and their passion for their research. Bernard seems to be driven by a craving for fame, not for the greater good of historical accuracy. Although few academics would snipe and banter quite as viciously as Hannah and Bernard, or be as nakedly ambitious as Bernard, nonetheless Stoppard is creating comedy by exaggerating something that certainly does exist in the real academic world.

Time has moved on between Acts 1 and 2. Two things have happened. Bernard has composed his lecture, in which he has constructed a false theory based on misinterpreting the 'evidence' he has amassed. And he has seduced Chloe, which explains her passionate defence of him from Hannah's interruptions and Valentine's light-heartedness.

Bernard claims he has uncovered a great historical scandal: Byron fought Chater in a duel because Chater had discovered Byron was having sex with Mrs Chater; Byron killed Chater and fled the country. Bernard believes this 'discovery' will make him an academic star. We hear a lot of his lecture, but he is increasingly interrupted. Only Chloe listens attentively, but she is more interested in the speaker than in his subject. Notice how from page 53 to 58 there is an increasing sense that Hannah and Valentine are not taking it seriously.

1809/2000 Hannah arrives with a copy of the letter we first learned about on page 26. There, Bernard gave a demonstration of his research acumen by suggesting the letter was from *Peacock* (Thomas Love Peacock, novelist and poet, 1785–1866). His guess has proved correct. It is ironic that he is right on this relatively small point but wrong about all the bigger ones.

Bernard manages to read two long extracts from the lecture (pages 53–4) which neatly lay out his version of what we know didn't happen! His speech on page 55 lays out how he has used the 'evidence' he found in Septimus's copy of Chater's book. We know all three notes were to Septimus, but Bernard assumes they were sent to Byron. **❍** Why is his line, *The covers have not survived,* so full of hidden meaning?

The crux of Bernard's mistake is laid out on page 56. He is convinced that if the letters had been to Septimus, the tutor would have removed them before loaning his book to Byron. **❂** How does he know it was Septimus's book?

Notice how Bernard's naked ambition is displayed on this page – *it's media Don, book early to avoid disappointment.* This desire for fame, and to 'get one over' on other researchers, clouds his judgement and causes him to make assumptions.

Bernard reveals another crucial misreading of the notes in his quote from his lecture at the bottom of page 56 to top of 57. He asks, *Did Septimus Hodge have any connection with the London periodicals?*, and answers himself: *No.* But we know that Septimus wrote the slanderous review of Chater's first book 'The Maid of Turkey'.

From this point to the explosion when *Bernard cracks* and *everything becomes loud and overlapped* at the top of page 58, Hannah tries to convince Bernard that his theory is unsound. Even though she thinks he is *arrogant, greedy and reckless*, she urges him to think again before 'going public'. But by now Bernard is flying too high to hear her. He has to be cajoled into not storming out. He finishes the lecture at the bottom of page 58 and waits for acclaim.

Hannah merely says, *Bollocks*. For most of page 59 she tries to persuade him to be more cautious in his assumptions. ✪ Do her arguments sound convincing, even if we did not know what actually happened in 1809?

Bernard's response is to attack Hannah's book on Caroline Lamb. Stoppard's stage note near the top of page 60 – *Things are turning a little ugly and Bernard seems in a mood to push them that way* – indicates how the mood of the scene must alter in a stage production. Imagine how body language and the grouping of characters might be used to show increasing tension between Hannah and Bernard, and how the row also engulfs Valentine.

✎ Valentine is disappointed that the lecture does not even mention the computer analysis of the reviews of Chater's books that he has done for Bernard. ✪ Why has Bernard left Valentine's findings out? Valentine's remark (page 60), *Well, it's all trivial anyway*, is like a red rag to a bull to Bernard. Valentine is coming from a science, not arts, background. He is claiming that it's knowledge, discoveries not personalities, that matter. But Bernard makes his living from analysing the work and personalities of writers and artists.

The focus of this dispute quickly widens into the familiar 'arts v. science' debate that raged for most of the twentieth century. By page 61 the atmosphere is too electric for anyone to suggest that perhaps art and science are separate disciplines with different ways of working. Bernard, having lashed out at Hannah's professional interests, now does the same with Valentine, whom he sees as a defender of scientific knowledge over artistic experience. After his first big speech on page 61, Bernard behaves unprofessionally, turning an academic argument into a personal one by saying (of scientists, and therefore, of Valentine), *I'd push the lot of you over a cliff.*

Bernard's second speech 'defending' his views (bottom of page 61) is different from his previous one. There the tone was lightly comic, with Bernard claiming to be quite happy with a world founded on outmoded scientific concepts and knowledge. But his second speech begins by posing a much more interesting idea: *If knowledge isn't self-knowledge it isn't doing much.* Although his tone is aggressive and dismissive (note how many **rhetorical questions** he asks), it is hard not to feel something for the passionate way in which he closes the beautiful quote from Byron by simply saying, *There you are, he wrote it after coming home from a party.* We might feel that he really is touched by the beauty of Byron's lines.

However, he ruins the effect by immediately mounting a spiteful attack on Valentine's far less dramatic research into grouse figures from the game books. The stage note at the top of page 62 reveals that Valentine is *shaking and close to tears.* Actors often portray him as a gentle and rather unworldly character, and he is clearly not used to this sort of attack. Furthermore he feels his own academic qualities undermined, because he is giving up on the game books research. He leaves, closely followed by the rest of the Coverlys, even Chloe: clearly a family who pull together in a crisis.

Bernard seems completely unaffected by the argument and by Valentine's tearful departure, saying simply, *It's no fun when it's not among pros is it?* Again Stoppard is satirizing the desire some academics have for starting arguments to prove intellectual superiority. ✪ How would you advise an actor playing Hannah to deliver her one-word reply to Bernard: *No?* What emotions or feeling should the word convey?

Even now, Bernard can't help but score a final intellectual point off Hannah. He appears to have proof that the picture she used on the cover of her book is not a portrait of Byron and Caroline Lamb. Hannah simply refuses to believe him. After all her arguing against Bernard and urging him to be careful, this is a complete reversal of her position. She appeals quite simply to knowing it is the right picture because she feels instinctively that it is. ✪ Compare this to Bernard's defence of *gut instinct*, which he claims Hannah lacks, on page 50. What might have caused Hannah to shift her position on having a 'feeling' for evidence? Did we ever explicitly know that she did not believe in *gut instinct*?

Apart from making a great literary discovery, Bernard's other passion appears to be attempting to seduce women. We already suspect he has made love to Chloe (something he confirms on page 64). Now, on page 63, he makes a sort of half-hearted attempt to persuade Hannah to come to London with him. He completely dismisses the lecture he has just spent the whole scene defending, in favour of sex. ✪ What might Stoppard be trying to indicate about Bernard's personality be such a sudden change of focus? How does this make you feel about him?

Sex remains the focus of the last few lines before Bernard leaves for London and fame. It is suggested that Hermione, Lady Coverly, is attracted to Bernard. But he has seduced the daughter, Chloe. He hardly registers the slap round the face he gets from Hannah when he says (of Chloe) *I saw something between her legs that reminded me of you*, suggesting that getting slapped might happen to him more than just now and again! Of course he is referring to the book he saw between Chloe's legs when she was up a library ladder in a none-too-subtle attempt to get Bernard to take an interest in her. The book contains a reference to the hermit whom Hannah plans to make the central figure in her new book. The effect of this last move on Bernard's part is to redeem, very slightly, all his previous bad behaviour.

As with some other scenes in *Arcadia*, Stoppard brings in the dramatic climax before the close of the scene, then winds down with a quieter, though dramatically vital passage. Here it is the return of Valentine and the refocusing of interest on Hannah's researches.

1809/ Two vital pieces of evidence are discussed. Bernard's find
2000 in the library tells us that the hermit lived in the garden hermitage for twenty years and had a tortoise as a pet. And the letter Hannah brought in at the start of the scene gives a picture of the hermit driven mad by trying to find a mathematical proof for a complex theory which Valentine identifies as the second law of thermodynamics. But the law had not been formulated when the hermit was living out his miserable existence.

The most important thing about the letter is that it gives dates: the hermit had the same birth year as Septimus. Hannah is beginning to get excited by the possibility that Septimus was an undiscovered genius who for some reason ended his days crazed and alone. She could be as excited as Bernard was about Byron fighting a duel. In fact Hannah's theory is correct in some respects but as crucially flawed as Bernard's in others, but she is keeping it to herself until she has definite evidence.
❂ What key fact about the hermit is Hannah getting wrong?

Test yourself

❓ Explain the double meaning of *genius* as used in this scene (on page 66), and earlier near the top of page 28.

❓ The letter from Peacock (page 54) is an example of historical facts being woven into the play. Peacock never wrote about the hermit because Sidley Park is a fiction, but his dates mean he could have sent a letter to Thackeray, who did edit the *Cornhill Review* in the 1860s. Find examples of other historical facts used in this scene. Then look elsewhere in the play for historical facts used to support the fiction. List or Mind Map what you find.

❓ On page 55, and again on 56, Bernard says *Where was I?* Each time the three members of his audience give short replies to prompt him. What do their replies indicate about their individual states of mind and preoccupations?

❓ Find the Mind Map you drew at the end of scene 2 showing the personalities of Bernard and Hannah. Add everything you have learnt or feel about each character from what has happened in this scene. Is there anything you put in after reading scene 2 that you now think is false? If so, remove it.

You may be a genius, but don't end up like Septimus! Take a break.

Scene 6 – 1809

◆ Septimus enters the house at dawn. He has shot a rabbit. Jellaby is bribed to report on the night's activities.

◆ Lady Croom enters with two letters. One is a love letter to her from Septimus. From her anger we assume it is very graphic.

◆ Jellaby brings a letter to Septimus from Byron.

◆ Lady Croom wants Septimus out, but he flatters her, and by the end of the scene she has ordered him to visit her room that evening.

◆ Septimus burns Byron's letter (which might have solved the twentieth-century mystery!).

Stoppard uses the term *reprise* in the opening notes for this scene. This means we see again the effects – 'dawn' lighting and distant pistol shot – that ended the first act (page 52). There, after the talk of duelling on page 42, we assumed the shot was a duelling pistol. Now from Septimus's comic entrance carrying a dead rabbit, we learn that the shot was only Septimus taking a pot-shot at the local wildlife.

✪ Imagine the scene change done on stage (look at the stage notes at the very start of the play if you need to remind yourself how the stage is set). What effects would you use to create the *reprise*?

This short scene breaks into two parts: Septimus's conversation with Jellaby, then his meeting with Lady Croom from where she enters at the bottom of page 68.

There is a considerable amount of 'action off', events we have not seen, reported by the butler. This first part of the scene should feature some physical comedy. Jellaby is the most senior servant in a great household; he is supposed to be stand-offish and cool by profession. Being handed a freshly killed rabbit is not the sort of thing he likes!

We don't know if Septimus slept in the boat-house to be ready to fight a duel at dawn, or to avoid fighting one altogether, or whether he knew from conversations (more 'action off') with Byron and Mrs Chater, that things might get ugly that night. Either way, he never explains his sleeping arrangements to anyone.

Septimus bribes the implacable Jellaby to tell him what has been happening to keep the house *up and hopping*. Brice has left with the Chaters. Byron has gone, taking Septimus's copy of Chater's book with him, but leaving Septimus with his pistols. The cause of these sudden departures was the discovery by Lady Croom of Mrs Chater leaving Byron's room at the dead of night. Presumably this was either very unlucky, or Lady Croom was on her way to visit Byron herself. Brice had brought the Chaters to Sidley Park (because he is infatuated with Mrs Chater) so Lady Croom threw him out with the Chaters. Byron was also given his marching orders. ✪ How might Byron's exit affect what happens at the end of this scene (or rather, at seven o'clock later that day)?

Lady Croom proves the truth of her earlier remark (page 13) about having the final word over her guests when she calls the dead rabbit a hare. Septimus corrects her, then corrects himself, after she has given him *one of her looks*: *No indeed, a hare, though very rabbit-like.*

This seemingly trivial exchange sets the tone for the most important meeting between the tutor and his employer in the entire play. What sort of look do you think she gives him? Is it just a stern gaze of authority, or might there be some humour, some self-awareness that she is playing a game? And when Septimus defers, but adds the sly rejoinder, is he engaging in a game too? Are they in fact flirting in a most surreptitious way? Remember that Lady Croom is in her mid-thirties, only ten or twelve years older than Septimus. They are both relatively young people.

Lady Croom orders her *infusion*, her tea, and holds court with Septimus while waiting for Jellaby to bring the complex apparatus that tea-making in grand houses involved in those days. The introduction of two more letters at this point might be a bit of devilment on Stoppard's part. While we accept Bernard's claim that people of this time wrote – *they scribbled – they put it on paper. It was their employment* (page 49), this is a play already crammed with vital notes. But the two that Lady Croom has opened and now presents to Septimus do not survive beyond this short scene.

They are both letters from him: one, a letter of unrequited love to Lady Croom, the other to Thomasina. Clearly Septimus did intend to fight the duel, and had considered the prospect of being killed. We don't know much of the content of the letter to Thomasina, but the reference to rice pudding and jam clearly shows he has remembered the wilder thoughts that the girl has shared with him. ❂ What does the act of writing the letter indicate about Septimus's feelings for his pupil?

Lady Croom is furious about the *most insolent familiarities regarding several parts of my body* in the letter to her, but throughout page 69 there is a sense of the mistress–servant divide collapsing. When Lady Croom says that the *sentence* is *banishment* she is giving herself the airs of a judge, but there is a strong sense that she won't carry out the sentence. Then, just before Jellaby brings the tea-making equipment, Lady Croom says something that Septimus knows is a lie. ❂ What is it, and why does she lie?

Lady Croom underlines the view she has of herself as mistress of the 'kingdom' of Sidley Park by referring to her decision to throw Septimus out as *banishment*. But at the bottom of page 69 she is beginning to slip into her trademark ironic wit. She wishes (though we begin to feel she does not entirely mean it) that Septimus and Chater had killed each other with the decorum due to a civilized house.

It is worth noting here that duelling, though not common and certainly illegal, was a recognized way for 'gentlemen' to settle disputes at this time. It was also possible for both duellists to be killed. If one man discharged his single-shot pistol and hit his opponent, who nonetheless remained standing, then the wounded man had the right to shoot at his unharmed opponent – who was obliged to stand still! Medical facilities were primitive, and the contestants could quickly bleed to death from relatively minor wounds caused by the *half-ounce ball* (page 42).

Jellaby brings yet another letter, from Byron to Septimus. The tutor now has two strong cards in his hand (Lady Croom's lie and a letter from someone to whom she was attracted), if only he knows how to play them. We assume he does not want to leave Sidley Park. He must find a way to

make Lady Croom allow him to stay. The balance of the scene swings totally from the middle of page 70, where Septimus gallantly makes Lady Croom's tea. She is keen to know what Byron has written to his good friend. Has he mentioned her in the letter? At the top of page 71, Septimus engages in some ridiculously over-the-top praise of Lady Croom, which flatters her. She first protests, *Oh really!* then *(protesting less) Oh really ….* She is softening, though she is taken aback when Septimus burns Byron's letter unread. It is worth imagining the value it might have had for Hannah and Bernard, whatever its contents.

Lady Croom is clearly fishing to find out how much Septimus thinks of Mrs Chater when she suggests that he will follow her to the Indies when he is thrown out of Sidley

Park. Septimus directs the conversation to Ezra Chater, who has been taken on as a botanist for an expedition organized by Brice. The real reason for Brice taking the completely untrained Chater is that Mrs Chater will come with him, *She will play mistress of the Captain's quarters*. Septimus cannot believe that Ezra Chater can be so easily deceived. Lady Croom's reply at the top of page 72 is both cutting and detailed. The two men may know Mrs Chater cheats on them, but they cannot help themselves, and choose not to recognize it. Lady Croom's second speech on that page sees her far less haughty, though still critical. She claims, revealingly for such a grand lady, to have experience of being betrayed before the ink has dried in a love letter. But being betrayed before the letter has even been composed, as Septimus has done by having sex with Mrs Chater, is a new experience for her. ✪ When Lady Croom implies she has been *betrayed* by Septimus, what shift in her thoughts are revealed?

Septimus seizes on her new mood and claims he only had sex with Mrs Chater to calm his *agony of unrelieved desire* for Lady Croom. Septimus could certainly lose his position now. But Lady Croom has made up her mind, she will have the tutor as a lover, however briefly. She spins the talk round to *drawers*, a daring sort of subject for a Lady to discuss with her servant in 1809! She makes it clear she does not wear them, and Stoppard writes in a brilliant stage note to underline what she is suggesting: *She turns with a whirl of skirts*. But even now she retains her air of authority. She does not timidly suggest a possible meeting. She orders him to come to her room, with a book for cover in case he is seen, where she can *spare him an hour* when she has bathed. In all things, even love-making, she is queen in her own house.

The scene ends with Septimus burning the two letters Jellaby brought him: vital historical evidence going up in smoke.

If you don't want your work to go up in smoke, don't burn the candle at both ends. Take a break!

Scene 7 – 1809 and Present day

Time has moved on in this scene, by three years for the 1809 characters and long enough for Bernard to make his discovery public.

◆ The Coverlys prepare for the dance. They wear 1809-style clothes.
◆ Valentine is using a computer to complete Thomasina's equations. It works.
◆ They identify Thomasina as the girl who died in the fire.
◆ Augustus is home from school. Septimus sets a drawing lesson.
◆ Thomasina's experimental mathematics is beyond Septimus.
◆ Augustus angrily reveals that he saw Septimus kissing Thomasina.
◆ Septimus gives Thomasina a scientific journal he is reading.
◆ Lady Croom despairs of the damage Noakes is doing to her garden.
◆ She reveals that Chater went to the Indies on a scientific voyage with his wife and Captain Brice. Mrs Chater became Brice's mistress. Chater discovered dwarf dahlias.
◆ Thomasina appears to have understood the complex physics in the journal.
◆ Lady Croom talks admiringly of Byron, whom she saw in London.
◆ Thomasina explains the Second Law of Thermodynamics.
◆ Augustus wants to know 'the facts of life'. Septimus obliges!
◆ Bernard arrives distraught. Hannah is going to publish her discovery of Lady Croom's notes on Chater's death, which destroy Bernard's 'duel' theory.
◆ Thomasina enters in a nightgown. It is the night before her birthday. She wants Septimus to teach her to waltz.
◆ Valentine realizes Thomasina's theory explains the basis of modern physics.
◆ Hermione has discovered Bernard and Chloe in the hermitage.
◆ Septimus and Thomasina dance. She begs him to visit her room. He begs her to be careful with her candle.
◆ Gus gives Thomasina's drawing of Septimus to Hannah.

This long scene has the two periods intertwining through it. You must read it very carefully to understand everything that is revealed or implied. Read the stage notes and try to picture the scene on stage. Stoppard is trying to create two worlds in one space, history coming alive but unseen by the modern characters.

Thomasina has been 13 years and 10 months up to now. In this scene she is on the eve of her 17th birthday. Time has also moved on for the contemporary characters, though probably just a few days – long enough for Bernard to have made his 'discovery' public and gained a lot of attention in the press. Stoppard may seem to overplay this a bit. Broadsheet newspapers might headline the story on their arts pages, but it is unlikely that a tabloid would run the headline *Bonking Byron Shot Poet* (page 74). ✪ Why might Stoppard deliberately exaggerate the interest in Bernard's claim here? What might he be making a sly dig at?

It is the day of the Coverly's dance. Chloe, Valentine and Gus are wearing Regency costumes. This is a visual device that, in a production, blurs the distinction between the 1812 and modern-day actors. Chloe is reading the newspaper reports of Bernard's discovery. She drifts into a speculation about the future. She believes everything is planned; that is, we live in a deterministic universe. Her comment (page 73), *Valentine, do you think I'm the first person to think of this?* echoes Thomasina's line on page 5, *Am I the first person to have thought of this?* ✪ Is Stoppard suggesting some link between the two young women? Is he hinting that the rather lightweight Chloe, whose chief function in the play is to be seduced by Bernard, could turn out to be a genius like Thomasina?

But Chloe soon returns to more personal matters by saying that sexual attraction appears to be the one thing that is random and uncontrolled in a deterministic universe. She is presumably thinking about her now famous seducer. This is underlined when she claims that Hannah is jealous of Bernard's success. Hannah appears to be just as detached and sceptical as ever, even as the house prepares to let its hair down for the dance. ✪ Do you think Hannah sounds older than she actually is when human affairs are discussed?

Compare her to Lady Croom: Hannah is the modern woman, Lady Croom the product of a society where women could not even vote. But who seems the more free?

Hannah is convinced that Bernard will get *the rug pulled from under him*; that is, his speculation about Byron and the duel will be proved completely false. After some banter which suggests that the joke about Hannah being Valentine's fiancée may, for Valentine, conceal an element of serious longing, they settle comfortably to their separate researches. Hannah is reading through Lady Croom's garden books, Valentine is using a laptop to work through Thomasina's equations.

As befits a pair whose main role in the play up to now has been intellectual rather than emotional, their moment of intimacy centres around Valentine's success with Thomasina's theory to create the *Coverly set*. Although Valentine says that the girl was on to something, he doesn't believe it means she was a young genius as Hannah supposes. It is then (bottom of page 76) we learn by implication the awful truth of what happened to Thomasina, of what will happen to her minutes after the play ends. ✪ At the very bottom of the page Hannah calls Valentine *Val*. What might this imply? Why might Hannah be changing her attitude to him at this point?

At the top of page 77, the first 'sharing of the stage' by characters from different eras occurs. Hannah and Valentine will allow the action to flow round them, as if they are invisible. The effect can be to suggest that Septimus, Thomasina and Augustus are the modern characters' thoughts given life. ✪ If you were directing a production of the play, what instructions would you give the actors playing Hannah and Valentine at this point? What unobtrusive things could they do while the nineteenth-century characters are on stage?

Thomasina is on the verge of womanhood. In her era, 17 was a very important age, when young girls became ladies to be introduced to 'good society' at balls and parties. The shift from childhood to womanhood, and to eligibility for marriage, was swift. But here she enters still childlike, chasing her brother.

Augustus is home from Eton, a great public school where boys of his social class were sent as boarders. Septimus seems unimpressed by this, however, and treats the young boy just as he does his long-term pupil. They settle to drawing. Septimus, with his usual show of indifference, tosses Thomasina's maths homework back at her. He admits he didn't follow her *rabbit* equation, her name for the theory she has invented which Valentine has just been working on. This is the first time we have seen the tutor admitting that his charge may be able to 'out-think' him. It is another facet of her coming of age.

Hannah shares the book with Septimus, *Septimus and Hannah turn the pages doubled by time*. It is a difficult piece of acting to pull off: remember the audience have to guess at the convention of how characters from the two eras share the stage. On page 78, Hannah, Valentine, Septimus and Thomasina take turns to comment on what is the beginning of Thomasina's grasp of something that later (in 'real' history) will be discovered and called the second law of thermodynamics.

It is important to understand some scientific history here. Isaac Newton (scientist and philosopher, 1642–1727) had formulated laws of physics which, in Thomasina's time, were accepted as the defining explanation of nature, motion: the whole universe. Key to this was the idea that motion or energy spent in one direction would create an equal force in return. But Newton failed to see that in any movement, heat is generated and lost. It follows that eventually everything will run down as there is less and less heat or energy available, since it is being lost in every action, every movement.

At the age of 13, Thomasina experimented with, but could not complete, iterated algorithms, which she maintained would be *a truly wonderful method whereby all forms of nature must give up their numerical secrets* (page 43). She was concerned purely with geometry. Now she is beginning to see the problem of heat lost in motion. This challenges Newton's laws, which in fact were not challenged until well after the 1809–12 setting of the events involving Thomasina's enquiring mind. Valentine's explanation to Hannah on page 78 sums up the science that you need to know to understand this part of the play.

*Valentine now accepts what he so far refused to believe: that Septimus was a genius and that some of his ideas rubbed off on his pupil. History is still being misread! But Valentine won't believe that the tutor was really onto something so fundamental that it could pre-date the disproving of Newton's laws. He says that scientific discoveries depend on one another and that such a momentous discovery could not have happened in a school room in Derbyshire because *You can't open a door till there's a house*: that is, the jump Septimus would have had to have made was just too big. There's an echo of the 'arts v. science' debate of pages 60–2 when Hannah quotes Byron (page 79) in defence of the genius of *lunatics and poets*. But here the disagreement is companionable, not confrontational.*

The great discovery Thomasina has made slips her mind. Soon she is joking with Septimus, saying that she might marry Byron. Childish squabbling between her and Augustus leads to her snobbish brother pulling 'aristocratic rank' on Septimus and storming out, again threatening to reveal his secret.

◕ Septimus's speech on page 80, beginning *I do not rule here*, may be yet another of the tutor's ironic explanations. But do you think he believes any of what he says?

The secret is that Thomasina told her brother that Septimus kissed her. Once again (as in scene 1) the setting for a liaison with sexual connotations is the garden, the hermitage which Noakes must have built in the years we have skipped across. But nothing in Septimus's attitude towards Thomasina in this part of the scene suggests he has any serious sexual feelings for her.

Count Zelinsky is a guest at Sidley Park, a piano teacher and tuner. ◕ What might explain the usually affable Septimus's apparent dislike of the Count, apart from having to listen to his piano playing!

Thomasina takes the scientific journal Septimus has been reading in which the ideas of a refutation of Newton's theories are contained. Septimus may be giving her the journal to shut her up, or he may know how gifted his charge is and be keen for her to read this report on cutting-edge scientific thought. Here, as throughout the play, we never really know what Septimus thinks of Thomasina's mental capabilities.

A long set of stage notes (pages 81–2) brings Lady Croom and Chloe back on stage. ✪ Why might Lady Croom, who has entered from the music room, appear *surprised and slightly flustered*?

There is a section on page 82 where characters from both eras interweave their conversations. Chloe and Valentine are looking for Gus; Lady Croom is searching for Noakes. Imagine this on stage. It highlights the complexities of the double time-scale that is operating throughout this scene.

Septimus's joke at the bottom of page 82 shows that he is not afraid to show his dislike of Count Zelinsky to his employer. But her aside, *Would you sulk?*, hints at greater freedoms: Septimus may be sulking because Zelinsky has replaced himself as Lady Croom's lover.

The stage note in the middle of page 83 that tells us *Hannah is caught by what she is reading*, is vital. She has seen something in one of the garden books, and will read it to Bernard on page 89. It is to be Bernard's undoing. Lady Croom explains it aloud: that Ezra Chater went to the Indies on a scientific voyage with his wife and Captain Brice. Mrs Chater became Brice's mistress, which was the plan all along. Ezra Chater discovered dwarf dahlias and sent the first specimens back to Sidley Park before dying from a monkey bite. Go back and read Bernard's comments about Chater the botanist on page 22. History has been misinterpreted once again.

Thomasina thumps the book down on the table, and interrupts her mother's thoughts on the death of Ezra Chater. Thomasina appears to have understood the contents of the article, and to be already thinking of bigger and more complicated possibilities for its theories. But the conversation on page 84 is overwhelmed by Lady Croom's and Septimus's flippancy. It is strange that Thomasina never demands to be taken seriously! ✪ Why do you think she is so accepting of the way she is treated?

As ever, Thomasina flits from one subject to another. She returns to her belief (we don't know if she takes it seriously herself) that she will marry Byron. Lady Croom and Septimus have seen Byron, now very famous, having his picture sketched by Fuseli. When Lady Croom says *Let him be hanged there for a Lamb*, she indicates that the poet was with Caroline Lamb. ✪ What does this remark suggest about Lady Croom's feelings?

The incident Lady Croom describes also tells us that the portrait Hannah used on the cover of her book on Lamb was the right one. Back on page 62, Bernard told Hannah that an expert had analysed the picture and dated it at *no earlier than 1820*. Another example of an expert getting it wrong.

We now return to events in the Arcadia that was the garden. Lady Croom lists what she sees as the horrors Noakes has clearly persuaded her husband to let him wreak in the garden. She hates the sound of the steam-driven pump and at the bottom of page 85 paints a comic but heartfelt picture of the destruction. Noakes, as ever, is completely outgunned by Lady Croom. He tries to explain that the *cowshed* is actually a hermitage.

Thomasina has produced a diagram developing the ideas she has just read. She uses Noakes's steam engine as an example of the second law of thermodynamics, which she appears to have worked out for herself. For the second time, Septimus is baffled by the intelligence of his pupil. Lady Croom, however, sees this not as a reason to praise her brilliant daughter, but as an indication that the need for a tutor is over. Lady Croom assumes her daughter will marry young, as she herself did.

On page 87, Septimus appears genuinely startled by what Thomasina has discovered. He is searching the article to find where it says that there will always be a loss of heat and energy. Thomasina's remark is in keeping with her tendency to jump from one idea to the next: *Nowhere. I noticed it by the way. I cannot remember now.* But she goes on to explain that the heat equation only goes one way, but that most people only *know it about engines*. She has seen that inevitable loss of energy applies to all motion. For the first time Septimus is being led by Thomasina's inquiring intelligence. And to end this exchange, she dashes off a good sketch of Septimus with Plautus the tortoise! (Everything in this play has a hidden meaning. Titus Maccius Plautus was a Roman comic poet.)

Thomasina leaves, a happy young woman, probably destined for genius. Immediately, Augustus enters and apologizes to

Septimus. Compared to his sister's inquiries, his are much simpler: he wants Septimus to tell him about 'the facts of life'. Thomasina has already told him what they are but he cannot believe what she says. ✪ How does she know them? What is suggested by Augustus wanting the sketch of Septimus?

There is a nice comment on sexual politics here. Augustus has gone to the grandest school in the land, but his horizons seem sadly limited compared with those of his sister, who has received her education 'only' from a hired tutor at home.

All the 1812 characters have left the stage clear for the conclusion of the modern-day part of the play. Bernard's agonized comment, *Fucked by a dahlia!*, immediately shifts the tone of the play to the present. On page 89, Hannah reads the entry in the garden book that *caught* her back on page 83. It proves that Chater was not killed at Sidley Park. ✪ Do you think Hannah's attempt to pacify Bernard by saying that Byron might still have fought Chater, just not killed him, is kindness, or a dig at Bernard's predicament.

Bernard thinks no one but Hannah knows about the dwarf dahlias. He wonders how long before he is caught out, and Hannah reveals she has sent a letter to *The Times*. If Hannah is gloating, she is doing it in her usual calm, detached manner. Her final line in the passage, where the flaw in Bernard's theory is explained (pages 89–90), is a classic put-down: *Think of it as a breakthrough in dahlia studies.*

Chloe gets Bernard into Regency costume for the photograph before the dance. In a production, this should provide a lot of visual comedy. Bernard doesn't want a costume, he wants a disguise. He may be over-reacting, but he believes the *media don*, will be hunted down and shamed by the same press that so recently celebrated him. In fact this is unlikely, but Bernard is a vain man convinced the whole world will want to relish his professional humiliation.

The modern characters go off for their photograph. The time moves to evening for both 1812 and the modern day. Septimus is up reading late when Thomasina enters furtively in her nightgown. She kisses Septimus passionately. Septimus is terrified: if Lady Croom even suspected she would throw him out, or worse! In fact, at this point Thomasina wants no more from Septimus than a dancing lesson. She may have worked out the principles of thermodynamics that afternoon, but all she can think about now is learning the waltz. She is a woman brimming with life waiting to be lived. This must be brought out in any production to add to the awful tragedy that befalls her.

Half-drunk, Valentine roots among the *considerable mess of papers, books and objects* on the table that both eras have shared throughout the play. He finds the diagram Thomasina drew after reading the scientific article (page 86). Septimus and he both study the diagram, locked in their separate worlds. Valentine has realized that Thomasina had drawn out the principle of heat exchange – she was a child genius. The theory ultimately leads to the end of the world, because there is no heat, no energy left. Both readers comment on the vision of the future that Thomasina's ideas lead to:

> Septimus: *So the Improved Newtonian Universe must cease and grow cold.* (page 93)
> Valentine: *And everything is mixing in the same way, all the time, irreversibly … Till there's no time left.* (page 94)

Thomasina's response to the inevitable decline of the universe that she has discovered is: *Then we will dance.* Septimus takes her in his arms, and they waltz.

While they dance, Bernard crashes in, tearing off his costume. Chloe follows, cursing her mother, who has discovered her and Bernard in the hermitage. He is going, and dismisses Chloe's invitation to go with him with a cruel, *Of course not. What for?* In contrast to this unkindness, we see Septimus kiss Thomasina: the second time, *in earnest.* Bernard makes theatrical apologies all round, and wishes Hannah good luck with her search for the hermit's identity. He is to be the central idea in her new book, 'The Genius of the Place'. Then Bernard makes his escape. ○ Why is Hannah's title so wrong? How many meanings can the word 'genius' have in her title?

Septimus tells Thomasina that she has mastered the waltz. She is now a young woman, and she wants him to come to her room. He refuses, and warns her to be careful with the flame of her candle. Tomorrow is her 17th birthday. They begin to dance again.

Gus, or could it be the ghost of Augustus, enters? (The stage note suggests that it takes a moment for us to realize it is Gus not Augustus when he stands at the door.) Gus somehow embodies the living spirit of the earlier age. His costume is *resplendent*, and his bow to Hannah is *regency*. This moment should contain a sense of magic, after all there are ghosts dancing round the now dimly lit stage. Gus gives Hannah Thomasina's sketch of Septimus with the tortoise. It has to be the same tortoise the hermit kept as a companion. Hannah now knows who the hermit was.

Gus and Hannah join the dancers from 200 years ago. Time is magically bridged. We know that in perhaps minutes Thomasina will die, and that Septimus will become a crazed hermit, vainly trying to prove what Thomasina so effortlessly discovered on this last day of her life. Gus and Hannah dance *awkwardly*, but Septimus and Thomasina dance *fluently*. In the plays' closing moments, the 'heartache for time never to be regained' (as one critic wrote) is almost unbearably tragic.

Test yourself

? Do you think more development of the relationship between Lady Croom and Thomasina would have added more humanity to the play, especially in the last scene? Does the play need it, or are the ideas more important than in-depth relationships between characters?

? Imagine you were watching the last moments of the play on stage. What do you think the dancing couples symbolize? Mind Map your ideas.

? Although the play has many very funny moments, it is a tragedy. Do you think the humour gives the tragedy more impact? Does Stoppard get the balance between laughter and sadness right? Make a Mini Mind Map of your ideas.

To waltz away with a grade A, take a break before reviewing what you've learned.

Arcadia was first staged in 1993. It was very well received by theatre critics. Stoppard is regarded as a major British dramatist and this play consolidated and enhanced his position. Using 'Stoppard' or 'Arcadia' as search queries, you can find several reviews of the play on the Internet.

Because it requires a large cast and is a complex play to stage, it is not often produced. And because (at the time of writing this guide) it has only been around for eight years, there is not a body of critical work to study. We can, however, look at one or two possible approaches for particular critical schools. These may give you ideas for your own assessment of the play.

Arcadia has very strong female lead characters and each one would give feminist critics a platform for comment. Thomasina could be regarded as a classic case of a woman of immense talent destroyed by a male-dominated society. Although this destruction is indirect (the cruellest way to look at her death is to say that she died by her own hand), it is a tragic irony that she dies possibly waiting for her tutor to come and make love to her. We never know if she accepts his refusal and goes quietly to bed, or if he will change his mind and go to her, but tragic events overtake the intentions of both characters. For all we know, Septimus could have been on his way to her room and discovered the fire himself.

Lady Croom is portrayed as a powerful woman, but we must note that ultimate power rests with her unseen husband. At the end of the day, Sidley Park is remodelled against her will. Her power and social position rest on the rank of her husband. On the other hand, she seems to choose her lovers as and when it suits her. She has chosen to be mistress of her own relatively small domestic world, rather than attempt to change anything in the wider one. But this world is created largely in the vacuum created by Lord Croom's apparent indifference to anything but shooting game.

Feminists would see Hannah as benefiting from changes in society that have occurred between the play's two time periods. She is more empowered. She represents a more balanced and professional approach to the study of history than Bernard. But Stoppard is also at pains to stress her lack of human warmth, and her inability to engage in the more frivolous things in life. (Notice that she won't take part in the dressing up or the photograph for the dance, and that when she comes on for the last time on page 92, Stoppard notes, *She has dressed for the party. The difference is not, however, dramatic.*)

It is up to you to decide whether this indicates a weakness or a strength in her character. However, a committed feminist might be critical of the fact that the (male) author of the play seems to be following a tradition, created by men, of saying that an intellectually serious woman must also be something of a boring human being. On the other hand, Hannah exhibits so much energy and vigour in the rest of the play, that it is hard to imagine Stoppard wanted us to see her as dull – she does threaten to kick Bernard in the balls (page 21)! Hannah may just be as cautious about life and commitments to other people as she is about her professional decisions.

Marxist critics, or those wishing to put a socio-economic spin on their reading of the play, would point to the presentation of the wealthy titled characters. No one in the play (except possibly Septimus) is actually impoverished, but it is the Crooms and Coverlys who are rich. Both families are portrayed as more than slightly eccentric, the Coverlys especially. More seriously, both could be said to be somewhat morally degenerate. It is suggested that both Hermione (Coverly) and Chloe go out of their way to make themselves available to Bernard. Lady Croom appears to have (or to try to have) sexual liaisons with Byron, Count Zelinsky and her daughter's tutor. It may sound puritanical to see this as some sort of 'degenerate' behaviour, but remember that in all these cases the men are officially in positions of duty or even subservience to Lady Croom.

Another more straightforward Marxist approach to the play would be to look at the balance of power through wealth. The

Crooms and Coverlys are extremely wealthy but seem to do little of any good or purpose with their money. They indulgence themselves creating or researching their gardens. Septimus, Hannah, even Bernard, have brains to spare compared to Sidley Park's various owners (with the possible exception of Valentine and of course Thomasina, who is too young, and too intelligent, to have the same 'adult' concerns and interests as the rest of the titled, land-owning set of characters).

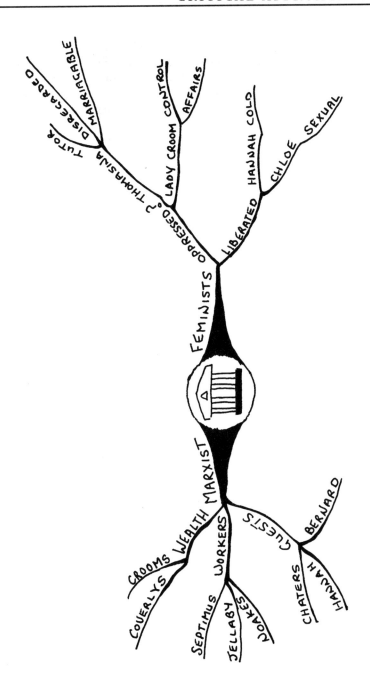

HOW TO GET AN 'A' IN ENGLISH LITERATURE

In *all your study, in coursework, and in exams, be aware of the following:*

- **Characterization** – the characters and how we know about them (e.g. speech, actions, author description), their relationships, and how they develop.
- **Plot and structure** – the story and how it is organized into parts or episodes.
- **Setting and atmosphere** – the changing physical scene and how it reflects the story (e.g. a storm reflecting chaos).
- **Style and language** – the author's choice of words, and literary devices such as imagery, and how these reflect the **mood**.
- **Viewpoint** – how the story is told (e.g. through an imaginary narrator, or in the third person but through the eyes of one character – 'She was furious – how dare he!').
- **Social and historical context** – the author's influences (see 'Context').
- **Critical approaches** – different ways in which the text has been, or could be, interpreted.

D*evelop your ability to:*

- Relate **detail** to **broader content, meaning and style**.
- Show understanding of the author's **intentions, technique and meaning** (brief and appropriate comparisons with other works by the same author will gain marks).
- Give **personal response and interpretation**, backed up by **examples** and short **quotations**.
- **Evaluate** the author's achievement (how far does she/he succeed – give reasons).

M*ake sure you:*

- Use **paragraphs** and **sentences** correctly.
- Write in an appropriate **register** – formal but not stilted.
- Use short, appropriate quotations as **evidence** of your understanding.
- Use **literary terms** correctly to explain how an author achieves effects.

Planning

You will probably have about 45 minutes for one essay. It is worth spending 5–10 minutes planning it. An excellent way to do this is in the three stages below.

1 **Mind Map** your ideas, without worrying about their order yet.
2 **Order** the relevant ideas (the ones that really relate to the question) by numbering them in the order in which you will write the essay.
3 **Gather** your evidence and short quotes.

You could remember this as the **MOG** technique.

Writing and checking

Then write the essay, allowing five minutes at the end for checking relevance, spelling, grammar and punctuation.

Remember!

Stick to the question and always **back up** your points with evidence in the form of examples and short quotations. Note: you can use '…' for unimportant words missed out in a quotation.

Model answer and plan

The next (and final) chapter consists of an answer to an exam question on *Arcadia*, with the Mind Map and plan used to write it. Don't be put off if you think you couldn't write an essay like this yet. You'll develop your skills if you work at them. Even if you're reading this the night before the exam, you can easily memorize the MOG technique in order to do your personal best.

The model answer and plan are good examples to follow, but don't learn them by heart. It's better to pay close attention to the wording of the question you choose to answer, and allow Mind Mapping to help you to think creatively and structurally.

Before reading the answer, you might like to do a plan of your own to compare with the example. The numbered points, with comments at the end, show why it's a good answer.

97

MODEL ANSWER AND ESSAY PLAN

QUESTION

How does scene 6 develop the action and characterization of the play, and how does Stoppard use different levels of meaning to convey important information?

Elements for a model answer. This question asks you to look at one scene, but relating it to the whole play. It also asks you to comment on how Stoppard uses language, so you will need to make some analysis of the text. You should consider how the balance of power between two of the main 1809 characters shifts, what this tells us about each character, and how it affects our understanding of the play.

You will find that making a Mind Map of the main elements you need to include in your answer will help you focus on the important points and stop you getting sidetracked by things that are not actually required to answer the question. Make the Mind Map before you begin writing the essay. It should look something like the one opposite:

ESSAY

'Arcadia' is a play in which every scene requires close reading to reveal all its levels of meaning. Scene 6 may appear to be the shortest and least important of the nineteenth-century scenes, but, as is often the case in this play, there is a huge amount of meaning behind the words.[1]

The scene shows Stoppard's grasp of humour, character development and plot movement. It shows Septimus and Lady Croom to have more than one dimension to their characters.[2] Up to now, she has been little more than a grand lady with a gift for cutting humour. Here she reveals her sexual side. Septimus has been seen principally as Thomasina's tutor. Although he has had an affair with Mrs Chater, we do not see this. Here he is alone with a woman for the only time in the play, and he reveals, under the usual wit and irony, a passion which we have not yet seen. Septimus is only 22, yet he

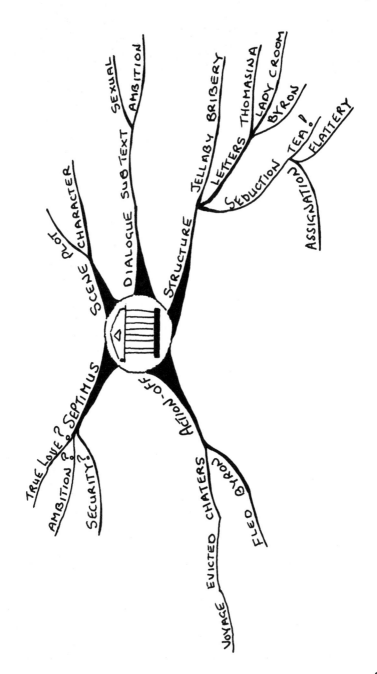

shows himself to be a skilled manipulator of the situation. His passion for Lady Croom may be something he has felt all along, or a ploy to flatter his employer and secure his continued position.[3]

It is never made clear exactly why Septimus has chosen to spend the night in the boat house. The conversation with Jellaby lets us know what has been happening during the night. There can be some physical humour when Septimus hands the dead rabbit to the stiff and formal Jellaby (who is probably wearing white gloves).[4]

Imagine Lady Croom's mood when she arrives. She has thrown her brother and the Chaters out, and been disappointed in an attempt to have a liaison with Byron. We don't know if she has any feelings for Septimus. She has to balance her private emotions with her public duty as the mistress of a house in which potential scandals have occurred.[5] Septimus's observation, 'A rabbit. No, indeed, a hare, though very rabbit-like,' is an attempt to humour and flatter Lady Croom. He is recalling her speech to Ezra Chater about the duty of guests to defer to the lady of the house on any matter.[6]

When Jellaby has gone, Lady Croom displays a rare show of genuine anger. She 'flings' onto the table two letters which Septimus has written. These were to her and Thomasina, to be opened if he was killed in the duel. She refers to hers as a 'love letter'. She calls Septimus a 'wretch', but this contains a hint of concern for him, not just anger at his daring to write the letter. She might be upset that he could have died without acting on his passions.[7] This must come as a shock: we have had no hint up to now that the relationship between her and Septimus could ever be more than mistress and employer.

She maintains her air of furious superiority over a tutor who dares to write 'the most insolent familiarities regarding several parts of my body'. The letter must be sexually explicit, certainly for the times in which it is written. On stage, her speeches through the bottom half of page 69 might be delivered with a dual edge: outrage, driven by a concern that a potential lover might have got himself killed. But her anger might also be driven by the fact that he was risking death over an affair with another woman.[8]

Lady Croom repeats in a more graphic way the events of the night, but with one telling alteration. She says it was Ezra Chater who discovered his wife creeping out of Byron's room. Septimus knows from Jellaby that she made the discovery. This was either chance (she just happened to be passing!), or she was on her own way to Byron's bedroom.[9]

Septimus now has an important card to play. The scene takes on the air of a game in which Septimus wants to win two things: continued employment at Sidley Park, and his mistress's affections. But we never know whether the second is really just a means of securing the first. He has never shown any hint of wanting her as a lover before, but then, like so many of the characters in this play, Septimus is a man who rarely reveals more than dry humour to the world. Either way, what happens between them is vital for setting up the background to the last scene of the play.

The 'tea-making' on page 69 is a cunning piece of stagecraft.[10] Lady Croom says she will make her own tea, unusual for a woman with servants to do everything for her. She wants Jellaby out of the way so she can talk privately to Septimus. Then Septimus takes over the tea-making. This is a physical demonstration of a probably slightly joking subservience. He has apologized for Byron's behaviour, and said that the poet will no longer be his friend. (If Lady Croom is throwing Septimus out, then of course she will have no idea if he will keep to this promise!)

The scene is becoming like a game of chess.[11] Certainly the two 'players' are skilled at not revealing their true feelings. Septimus risks a bold move at the top of page 71 when he voices extravagant praise for Lady Croom. It works: she is flattered. Her three 'Oh really's' on page 71 should be delivered on stage to show (1) comic outrage at Septimus's exaggerated praise, (2) genuine appreciation of the flattery, (3) shock at the burning of Byron's note. The note turns to ash, perhaps a symbol of the end of Lady Croom's interest in Byron, leaving the possibility that Septimus might replace him.

Septimus's ironic line, 'Now there's a thing – a letter from Lord Byron never to be read by a living soul,' remind us of the other time-scale of the play, and of the vital evidence that has just gone up in smoke. If Bernard could have found that letter, he might never have made his disastrous assumptions.[12]

This is underlined by Lady Croom talking about the Chaters sailing to the Indies with Brice. We have already heard Bernard dismiss the reference in the British Library database to a Chater who died in Martinique (page 22). Now we know that this was the same Chater, and that Bernard has made another fatal error.

Lady Croom provides more information about events that are vital to the plot but which we will not see. Brice is infatuated with Mrs Chater and has set up the post of botanist for the completely unqualified Ezra Chater, only so that his wife will come on the voyage and 'play mistress in the Captain's quarters'. Poor Ezra is about to be deceived again!

The conversation about the Chaters leads into Lady Croom's cunning and comic observation about men duelling over women. She and Septimus appear to converse not only as equals, but as a couple who share a similar ironic view of the world. They seem well matched. Perhaps this spurs Lady Croom's decision to take Septimus as a lover. Perhaps Septimus is not only attractive to her because he is young, but also because he is intelligent and witty, a match for her own way of talking and joking.[13]

She returns to the 'love letter', but with none of the anger she previously showed. Indeed she makes a joke about having been deceived in love by men who broke promises they wrote to her 'before the ink is dry', but finds Septimus's affair with Mrs Chater, a deception upon her carried out before the letter was even written, a new experience. The joke has a hidden meaning. She is suggesting that she feels betrayed, that she has had thoughts about Septimus that could be betrayed. Septimus knows from this that he has 'won the game'. All he has to do now is continue to denigrate Mrs Chater, and praise Lady Croom.[14]

He seems to have no fears about what a liaison with his employer might mean in the future. He derides Mrs Chater and praises Lady Croom by saying, 'I thought in my madness that the Chater with her skirts over her head would give me the momentary illusion of the happiness to which I dared not put a face.'

Lady Croom closes the scene in a way that leaves Septimus in no doubt why he is going to her room later, and that, when 'she turns with a whirl of skirts', she is not wearing any knickers! She has regained total command of the situation, but by using her sexuality not just her position. But even here, Stoppard never allows his characters to speak directly about their intentions.[15]

The tone of the end of the scene contrasts with the way the twentieth-century researchers might be tempted to see these figures from history. It shows the 1809 characters to be as passionate and vital as the modern-day ones. They are literally history coming alive. It is a shame that Hannah and Bernard will never be able to share the view of them that we in the audience enjoy.[16]

WHAT'S SO GOOD ABOUT IT?

1 Ability to locate the scene within the plot of the play and to see its importance.
2 Ability to see through the 'surface' of the dialogue to the deeper meaning of the scene.
3 Good grasp of the characters as they have been revealed in the play.
4 Insight into how the play might be performed.
5 Shows an understanding of the nineteenth-century setting of the play.
6 Ability to make connections between details in this scene and close reading of other parts of the play.
7 Evidence of close reading and of possible interpretations.
8 As for point 7.
9 Understanding of the implications of 'evidence' presented in the text.
10 Insight into how the text is enhanced by performance.
11 Shows a sophisticated reading of Stoppard's way of writing scenes.
12 Shows understanding that the details of this scene have importance for the twentieth-century element of the play.
13 Reveals in-depth understanding of characters.
14 Shows clear understanding of the way the scene is structured speech by speech.

15 Refers back to the question, relating the action of the close of the scene to the way Stoppard uses language.

16 Good conclusion which does not simply repeat what has come earlier. Final sentence presents a valid personal response showing both appreciation of the play and an awareness of the relationship between characters and audience.

GLOSSARY OF LITERARY TERMS

absurdity (absurd humour)   absurd humour turns on an idea or situation being so out of the expected, of things being so out of any usual harmony, that the result is comic.

action off   events that are imagined to take place during the time-scale of the play, but which do not happen on stage. They are usually reported by one or more characters.

alliteration   the repetition, for effect, of consonant sounds at the beginning of words or syllables.

allusion   the use of literary, cultural and historical references.

assonance   the repetition, for effect, of vowel sounds.

backstory   information about the characters or plot, provided (in dialogue) so that the audience can understand the action.

caricature   exaggeration and simplification of character traits.

characterization   the way in which characters are presented.

context   the background of social, historical and literary influences on a work.

dialect   regional form of language varying from the standard in vocabulary and grammar.

diction   choice and arrangement of words.

didactic   intended to instruct; in literary criticism, often used in a negative sense.

discursive   presenting a logical argument, step by step.

farce   a form of comic stage drama characterized by misunderstandings, people hiding from one another on-set, and usually driven by a plot involving illicit sexual liaisons.

Feminist criticism   critical approach based on assessing the role of gender in texts. A particular issue is the subordination of female characters in patriarchal societies.

genre   type of literary work conforming to certain expectations; e.g. tragedy.

idiom   a characteristic expression of a language or **dialect**.

image a word picture bringing an idea to life by appealing to the senses.

irony a comic device whereby a character really means the opposite of what their words apparently express. It is normally used to be sarcastic or to ridicule.

Marxist criticism critical approach which sees literature in relation to class struggle, and assesses the way texts present social realities.

metaphor a compressed **simile** describing something as if it were something else.

paradox an apparently contradictory statement which contains some truth; e.g. 'I hear her hair has turned quite gold from grief' (*The Importance of Being Earnest*).

parody an exaggerated copy (especially of a writer's style) made for humorous effect.

persona an assumed identity.

personification describing something (a place, an object) as if it were a person or, less often, describing someone as embodying the spirit of a place, thing or ideal.

picaresque type of novel popular in the eighteenth century, featuring the adventures of a wandering rogue; e.g. *Tom Jones* by Henry Fielding.

plot the storyline, the events that take place and the sequence in which they occur.

polemical (of style) making an argument.

rhetorical questions a question asked by someone who wants to provide the answer themselves. Often used in speeches to draw in the audience's attention.

sarcasm any bitter or cutting comic remark that is not just a blunt insult.

satire literature which humorously exposes and ridicules vice and folly.

simile an **image** comparing two things similar in some way but different in others, normally using 'like' or 'as'.

subplot subsidiary plot coinciding with the main plot and often reflecting aspects of it.

themes   the ideas, beliefs or issues that underlie the events of the plot.

tone   the mood created by a writer's choice and organization of words; e.g. persuasive.

viewpoint   the way a narrator approaches the material and the audience.

wit   an amusing remark involving a mixture of brilliance and surprise. It is a light type of comedy, though it can also be loaded with venom.

word-play   using the potential for double meaning in words or phrases to comic effect.

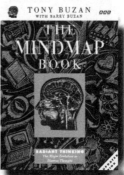